Why Boys Don't Talk and Why We Care:

A Mother's Guide to Connection

Susan Morris Shaffer

Linda Perlman Gordon

Mid-Atlantic Equity Consortium, Inc.

The Mid-Atlantic Equity Center of the Mid-Atlantic Equity Consortium, Inc.,
is funded by the U.S. Department of Education under Title IV of the Civil Rights Act of 1964.

The content of this publication was developed under a grant from the
Department of Education. However, the opinions expressed in this publication
do not necessarily reflect the position or policy of the U.S. Department of Education,
and no referral endorsement by the Department of Education should be inferred.

Publication design by Jill Tanenbaum Graphic Design & Advertising, Inc.

How to Order This Book
By Phone: 301-657-7741
By Fax: 301-657-8782
Online: www.maec.org
Mid-Atlantic Equity Consortium, Inc.
5454 Wisconsin Avenue
Suite 655
Chevy Chase, Md 20815

This book is dedicated to our sons,
Zachary and Seth,
and our daughters,
Emily and Elizabeth,
for teaching us the importance of connection.

Acknowledgments

We are grateful for the encouragement, personal stories, and enthusiasm of so many friends and colleagues who have given us the support that has made this book possible.

Thank you to our families — Arnie, Zach, Emily, Mark, Seth, and Elizabeth.

To our colleague Sheryl Denbo for her candor, care, and critiquing of the manuscript.

To our colleagues Lynson Moore Beaulieu and Charo Basterra for their insights and honesty, especially for their participation in the chapter "Focus on Adolescent Males of Color."

To all the parents, teachers, administrators, and teenage boys and girls who shared their personal stories with us and to those who invited us into their homes to take photos.

To Sandy Kavalier for her skills in capturing the truth about boys' lives in the photos we've chosen for the book.

To Stephanie Downey who started the project with us and participated in much of the original research.

To our copy editor Jean Bernard for her attention to detail and commitment to the project.

To Jill Tanenbaum, Sue Sprinkle, and Teri Watson for translating our words with such creativity and accessibility.

To those who have given us valuable input throughout the project: Christine Stimpson, Ray Yau, Donna Shoom-Kirsch, Susan Wechsler, Janine Perlman, Wilma Bonner, Helen Pearson, and parents who graciously gave us permission to use their children's images.

To Lee Canter for encouraging us to use our own voices.

To Shawn Oberrath, our research associate, for her intelligence and commitment, and for being a joy to work with.

To Lynn Levinson for her ability as a teacher and mentor to inspire and connect with adolescent boys.

Finally, to our friend Tricia Segall Davis, who never ceases to inspire us with her love of life and for bringing out the best in our sons.

Susan Morris Shaffer and Linda Perlman Gordon
March 1, 2000

Mother to Son

Well, son, I'll tell you:
Life for me ain't been no crystal stair.
It's had tacks in it,
And splinters,
And boards torn up,
And places with no carpet on the floor—
Bare.
But all the time
I'se been a-climbin' on,
And reachin' landin's,
And turnin' corners,
And sometimes goin' in the dark
Where there ain't been no light.
So, boy, don't you turn back.
Don't you set down on the steps
'Cause you finds it's kinder hard.
Don't you fall now—
For I'se still goin' honey,
I'se still climbin',
And life for me ain't been no crystal stair.

—Langston Hughes

From COLLECTED POEMS *by Langston Hughes. ©1994*
by the Estate of Langston Hughes. Reprinted by permission of Alfred A. Knopf,
a Division of Random House, Inc.

Left to right:
Zachary Gordon
Susan Morris Shaffer
Linda Perlman Gordon
Seth Shaffer

Introduction

This book seeks to answer the question, "Are there better ways to raise our boys?" Our intended audience is parents of boys. The book is written from our personal experience as mothers of teenage boys and as professionals in the fields of gender and adolescent issues. We are, professionally, a gender equity specialist and a clinical social worker who, together, have more than 30 years of experience working on gender issues. As mothers of two daughters and two sons, each of us discovered that raising our teenage sons was turning out to be a very different experience from raising their older sisters. We began to have conversations about our shared experiences. We realized through these discussions that the range of emotional expression for boys was limited, and we felt the need to broaden their options and experiences. This challenge became especially clear to us as both of our sons progressed through their teenage years.

We have woven our own experiences, as well as those of other parents, boys, girls, and professionals in the field, throughout the book. In addition, we have included a thorough review of current research and information, including statistical evidence; recent studies from the social and scientific disciplines of psychology and biology; information from popular culture; and individual case studies. This research is provided because we believe that it is important to help parents understand the intellectual foundation of many of the misconceptions about boys that are prevalent in our society. New information demonstrates that we can improve how we raise our boys.

Our intent is to present parents with a practical guide, including strategies to increase the emotional dimensions and opportunities for connection with our boys. We know that specific chapters of the book will be of more interest to you than others, but we encourage you to read the book in its entirety, because there are important lessons to be learned in every chapter. Throughout the book we attempt to look at boys from a cross-cultural perspective, acknowledging that the existing literature and research tend to have a White, middle-class bias. While our focus groups represent a sample of Latino, African American, Asian, and European American boys, many of the issues that adolescent boys face are similar across diverse races and socioeconomic classes. For this reason, we have not identified quotes from boys according to race or ethnicity, except in chapter 6, where we focus exclusively on males of color. However, some issues are unique to one group or are emphasized by the conditions of an individual cultural or racial group. It is not uncommon for diverse groups of boys and parents to respond to issues differently as well. This reality is the reason for our separate discussion of males of color.

What was reinforced for us and helped to guide our perspective throughout the writing of this book is the desire of mothers to stay close to their sons during the teenage years. After meeting with mothers of African American, Asian, European American, and Latino boys, it became clear that there are as many differences within each group of boys as there are between the groups. Among the sons, some are reserved, others are outgoing; some are good writers, athletes, scientists, computer whizzes, performers; some do well in school, others do not; some are leaders, others are followers. What these mothers have in common is that they love their sons and want to know them better. Ultimately, it is our aim to provide parents from a wide variety of cultures with the confidence to find their own voice, trust their instincts, and maintain emotional connections with their sons.

Chapter 1

Why Boys Don't Talk and Why We Care

We care because when boys don't talk, we assume that they don't feel.

We care because when boys don't talk, we don't get to fully know them; we end up validating only one part of them.

We care because when boys don't talk, it inhibits intimacy.

When we leave boys alone, we shortchange their emotional growth; as a result, part of boys remains hidden. Just as we were sensitized and motivated to change the landscape for girls, and just as we helped to expand the options available to girls, our personal experiences with our sons and their friends has helped us to understand that the next challenge is to focus on boys.

Recently, an explosion of academic research and popular literature has focused public attention on how we raise and educate boys in our society. Harvard researcher Carol Gilligan recognizes that, "Boys feel they have to separate from women, and they are not allowed to feel that separation as a real loss…. What we are finding out is how vulnerable boys are. How, under the surface, behind the psychic shield, is a tender creature who's hiding his humanity" (Norman, 1997).

We have made so much progress in deconstructing obstacles for girls, and we are really at the earliest stage of deconstructing obstacles for boys. —*Focus Group Parent*

ZITS　　　　　　　　　　　　　**BY JERRY SCOTT AND JIM BORGMAN**

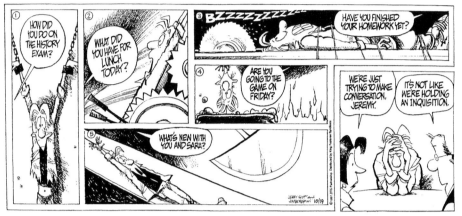

Reprinted with special permission of King Features Syndicate.

We believe that boys don't talk because they think it's safer not to talk. When we spoke with boys in the focus groups, it became clear to us that when boys reveal their vulnerability, they fear being perceived as weak. Expressing oneself is risky and exposes a boy to many reactions and interpretations. In fact, in our focus groups with boys, many of them explicitly stated that they do not go to their parents with problems for fear of being misjudged and permanently labeled. Instead, boys protect themselves by frequently trying to solve their issues on their own.

Every parent and teacher has had experience with boys trying to solve problems on their own. This response is the boys' attempt to create a face-saving silence, which takes the form of one-word answers and fools us into thinking that our boys are doing well and don't need or welcome our intervention. When parents experience this behavior, it is difficult to know how to proceed. One father with whom we spoke remarked: "There is more communication with daughters so that I feel like even if I say something 'wrong' on Tuesday, we'll be chattering enough during the week so that we can fix it. With boys, you basically have to do it in three sentences or less and, at the most, that will be twice a week. There is no recovery opportunity. Rather than talking, I find myself trying to figure out the right thing to say." Parents of teenage boys know there is a lot of pressure to

Living with a teenager is living with an intimate stranger, and parents are left to puzzle through when to step in and when to let go. — Lisa Belkin, "Getting the Girl"

say the ***right*** three sentences. It is, therefore, not surprising that parents so often don't know what to say. To improve our connection with our sons, we must first understand that when boys don't talk, it is a way of protecting and preserving oneself. It should not be interpreted as disinterest or a lack of need for emotional involvement.

It has become increasingly apparent to those of us in education and mental health that the range of acceptable outlets for boys is much narrower than it is for girls. It's interesting to hear the point of view of girls in our focus groups, because unlike boys, they feel that they have a wide range of activities and emotions to engage them. One girl even stated, "There is a wide range of what girls can do as opposed to guys, like singing and dancing. Girls can do any of that stuff without anybody judging." Boys, on the other hand, talk about far fewer activities. In fact, the U.S. Department of Education reports that boys participate almost exclusively in one category of extracurricular activity — team sports — at the expense of participation in any other type of school club or affiliation (U.S. Department of Education, 1996b; National Urban League, 1998).

As parents, our challenge is to reach boys in a way that is compatible with their need to save face, while encouraging growth and creating connections. We have to learn to "get" to boys in such a way that they will actually hear us. If the avenues available for full emotional expression for boys are very limited, how can we (loving parents and teachers) reach them? How can we facilitate our boys' struggles to become men while expanding their narrow options for affiliation? Parents and teachers must walk a thin line between asking their boys to grow up and be independent men, and wanting them to value the personal and familial relationships that are defined as connectedness. Ultimately, we want them to achieve this balance, not only as teenagers, but as emotionally connected men as well. Although it's acceptable to prepare boys for the role of provider and the world of work, we haven't focused on

> My son is not good at sports. He would be a very good actor, but he doesn't want to go to any drama or acting classes. He refuses. He goes to sports camps, even though he doesn't like it. I feel so sad for him. I made him try out for drama club because he has a great voice, and he was deliberately terrible.
> —*Focus Group Parent*

the importance of preparing boys to build and sustain relationships, such as marriage and parenting. Creating and supporting this balance will only enhance a man's ability to perform in the world of work and appreciate and sustain lasting relationships (Kimmel, 1999).

New research from Harvard Medical School and the Stone Center at Wellesley College points out that walking this thin line isn't inherently necessary. In fact, the pressure that many mothers feel to push their sons away is not a natural phenomenon. It is created by cultural messages received by the mother and son that say men should be "strong, competitive, aggressive, and unfeeling" (Meltz, 1998). This research argues instead that mothers should encourage emotional closeness with their sons. Not only is this something boys want, it's something they need. Fathers and other adult male mentors also need to stay close to their boys emotionally and support them in staying close to their mothers. We love our sons, but we still may fail to create strong connections or to build a structure of obligations and responsibilities, emotional or practical, for participation in family life. One mother expressed, "There's a connection between having the male child participate in the family and have responsibilities in the family. The male arrogance that I see is a result of not having responsibilities in the family." The question becomes: How can we help teach our kids these skills so that when (and if) they become fathers, they can instruct their sons?

> They can become men who express their emotions and treat their partners respectfully, who listen as well as act, and who love and nurture their children. —*Michael Kimmel, "What Are Little Boys Made Of?"*

Why boys won't talk is further rooted in the interplay of culture, biology, and psychology. Why do we care? We care because the disconnectedness of boys has led to a near epidemic of undiagnosed male depression, suicide, and — among both middle- and lower-income boys — violence against each other and women. Psychologist William Pollack, a professor at the Harvard Medical School and director of the Center for Men at McLean Hospital in Boston, describes the following phenomenon:

When boys repress feelings like love because of social pressure, "They've lost contact with the genuine nature of who they are and what they feel. Boys are in a silent crisis. The only time we notice is when they pull the trigger" (Pollack, 1998). Too frequently violence becomes one of the very few means boys feel they have to express emotions. We have seen evidence of this in the rapid escalation of shootings in our schools and in our homes. When boys lack a full range of affiliations and emotional expressiveness, they often turn to competitive models defined by winning or losing. By allowing competition to be one of the few acceptable models for expression of emotion, parents and educators undercut boys' ability to succeed in a variety of areas. In addition, boys begin to think of themselves as "winners or losers," and those who are labeled as "losers" can become dangerous to themselves and others.

The effect of this model is that we have very few acceptable markers of manhood. It becomes difficult for boys to know when they become so-called real men. This is demonstrated primarily by the manner in which

SURVEY OF THE HEALTH OF ADOLESCENT BOYS

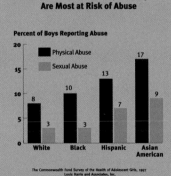

Asian American and Hispanic Boys Are Most at Risk of Abuse

Percent of Boys Reporting Abuse

The Commonwealth Fund Survey of the Health of Adolescent Girls, 1997
Louis Harris and Associates, Inc.

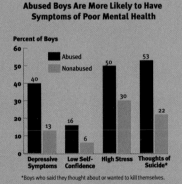

Abused Boys Are More Likely to Have Symptoms of Poor Mental Health

Percent of Boys

*Boys who said they thought about or wanted to kill themselves.

The Commonwealth Fund Survey of the Health of Adolescent Girls, 1997
Louis Harris and Associates, Inc.

One in eight male high school students has been physically or sexually abused. Rates of abuse varied by mothers' education, and by the boys' race and ethnicity. Those from families in which the mother had less than a high school education were more than twice as likely to report abuse than those from homes in which the mother was a high school graduate. Asian American and Hispanic boys reported higher rates of abuse than did Whites and African Americans. Boys who reported being abused also displayed symptoms of poor mental health at a higher rate than did boys who were not abused. In addition, the survey found that one in five adolescent boys did not receive physical health care when needed. At least one in four Black, Hispanic, and Asian American boys reported not having a regular health-care source, compared with 17 percent of White boys. —*The Commonwealth Fund, "Survey of the Health of Adolescent Boys"*

> What these recent school shootings reveal is not a crisis in youth culture but a crisis in masculinity. The shootings — all by White adolescent males — are telling us something about how we are doing as a society, much like the canaries in coal mines, whose deaths were a warning to the miners that the caves were unsafe.
> —*Jackson Katz and Sut Jhally, "The National Conversation in the Wake of Littleton is Missing the Mark"*
>
> If we understand the sadness in boys, we'll deal with that sadness and not have to wait to have to cope with their aggression.
> —*James Garbarino, Lost Boys: Why Our Sons Turn Violent and How We Can Save Them*

boys compartmentalize their emotional lives. They value toughness and a macho facade, and emotional connections are viewed as unsafe and threatening. Because of the constraints of socially acceptable forms of emotional expression, it takes a lot of time and effort to see behind their male bravado. This bravado frequently hides emotions and gives the false impression that everything is just fine, making it difficult to pinpoint male problems. In contrast, we are generally more aware of the problems of girls because they often display their emotions on the surface and come to us with their troubles.

Our society teaches us that men and boys are less in need of friends, social bonds, and connections. Consequently, boys learn to hide their desire for these things. This situation leaves parents without the means to stay close to their sons. As a result, parents tend to be harsher with boys than with girls to keep them in line. To avoid these restraints, boys find ways to hide their feelings. Too often a boy's sense of identity, to a greater extent than a girl, is based on separation from his parents and on denying his feelings. This often leads to a form of alienation.

One psychologist, Susan Wechsler, worries about "how easy it is for some boys to disconnect themselves from others. It seems more than simple independence and has a more negative feel to it...." Another psychologist, Donna Shoom-Kirsch, believes that, "This alienation permits disrespect and the blaming of others. It also fuels apathy, lack of empathy, and may contribute to the increase of violence in schools."

If we raise our boys to have a lack of empathy, it makes sense that they won't be averse to inflicting violence on others. As therapists tell us, one of the most important things that we as parents can do is to increase our child's capacity for empathy, and to help the child to understand what it's like to be in the position of another person whom the child or others are abusing (Pollack, 1998). For example, those boys who have experienced racism and can talk about it are also better able to understand sexism as oppression of another group. All boys have some personal experience that can help them to empathize with others.

> I want to mention that one of the most salient things that I noticed about boys and men was the degree to which there was a preoccupation with weak versus strong. It's not too difficult to see how quickly that evolves into a predisposition to prove one's strength by means of violence, particularly if a child doesn't have nonviolent means available to show that he is strong.
> —*James Gilligan, Violence: Reflections on a National Epidemic*

While one assumes that White boys, in particular, grow up to obtain superior opportunities and power, studies show that a large percentage of boys, in general, comprise the lowest sector of school performance. So, while it is acknowledged that boys comprise the high end of test scores, it's not as widely known that they also dominate the low end (Bushweller, 1994). Boys' discipline problems, which certainly affect achievement, may be caused, in part, by their disconnectedness in school. While the origin of that disconnectedness may be related to both gender and race, acting out in school is the kind of behavior that leads to academic failure. It also hinders the process of achieving maturity and social integration.

> If we raise our boys to have a lack of empathy, it makes sense that this results in violence. —*William Pollack, Real Boys: Rescuing Our Sons from the Myths of Boyhood*

Instead of promoting connection, our society dictates that separation is the primary focus of boys' psychological development (Siegler, 1997).

Boys do not ache for their fathers' masculinity. They ache for their fathers' hearts.

— Terrence Real, I Don't Want to Talk About It: Overcoming the Secret Legacy of Male Depression

Independence is almost enshrined in American culture. From a psychological perspective, our historical model has been "Boys will be boys." Parents have followed the tradition of pushing boys to separate from them so they will become "healthy" male adults. Many parents believe that remaining connected to family inhibits the development of the so-called autonomy needed to be masculine. According to Dr. William Pollack (1998), "We prematurely separate boys from their mothers and nurturing in general in a way we don't do to girls. And we call that normal male development, and my argument is that not only isn't it normal, but it's traumatic, and that trauma has major consequences."

Our need to enshrine independence has been at war with the basic human need for love, support, and emotional encouragement. In fact, "Boys do not long for fathers who will usher them through the gauntlet of psychological disconnection. They long for fathers who have themselves survived intact. Boys do not ache for their fathers' masculinity. They ache for their fathers' hearts" (Real, 1997).

In an encouraging new development, many respected professionals have turned their attention to the psychological development of boys and have reframed the adolescent task of separating in a way that is more consistent with our instincts about the value of connectedness. This new psychological model holds that parental love is not the enemy of healthy male development. Parental love is not the all-powerful relationship that needs to be severed so that the adolescent boy can grow into an independent adult. In other words, male maturity is not shamed or emasculated by having a parent or parents who want to remain competent and close.

We often find that theories of biology are at odds with psychological and cultural models of adolescent male development. Many scientists and academic researchers argue that, biologically, boys are "hard wired" and hormonally equipped to behave aggressively (Gurian, 1996). If this is true, and if it has been necessary for the survival of the species, why is there so little documented evidence of violence and aggression among Amish men and boys (Garbarino, 1999)? Given the statistical reality, however, that boys' safety is in peril, is it possible to change our boys' behavior by the way we raise them?

We agree with Carol Gilligan when she states that research on boys is an extension of the work that we have been doing with girls (Norman, 1997). The issues associated with providing our children with more models for emotional expression are not a matter of boys versus girls. Children of both genders must be able to reach their full potential with a complete range of emotional expressiveness. The new research shows that we need to place value on attachment as the primary task of human growth, for both boys and girls, because without community and closeness we fail to thrive as individuals and as members of society, regardless of our gender, race, or social class.

With some boys acting out in the classroom, and many men operating in an emotional vacuum, parents and educators wonder: Is there an appropriate, integrative emotional model for boys? We think there is, and we hope that this book provides you with a model you can use.

In the chapters that follow, we use case studies taken from our focus groups and conversations with teenage boys and girls (ages 14–16), mothers, fathers, coaches, counselors, teachers, and psychologists to outline issues, provide strategies for parents, and identify resources for increasing the ways in which boys can connect and still become men. We provide you with tools to support the growth of emotional intelligence in boys, and explain why the interplay of those values in our culture that forgive, if not encourage, antisocial behavior and disconnectedness among boys fail them and society as a whole.

Why do we care? We care because statistics prove that many of our boys are at risk, and society suffers as a result. We have seen recently what can happen when boys are disconnected from their families, schools, and peer groups. The following description by two psychologists explains some of the elements in society that teach violence and may have acted as catalysts in the Columbine High School killings and other tragedies. They maintain that any apprentice needs four things to learn his or her trade: role models, tools, social validation, and opportunities to practice.

1. Violent media (including the news) constantly show heroes engaged in war and killing.

2. Guns and assault weapons are widely available for sale.

3. Internet sites that illustrate bomb-making provide validation and legitimization from a broader community of online Internet users.

4. Opportunities to practice are available in violent video games.

None of these individual factors caused the overwhelming tragedy that occurred at Columbine. But given the motivation developed by years of peer victimization, and the absence of parental oversight, the culture provided all the elements of an effective apprenticeship in the practice of war (Greenfield and Juvonen, 1999). As President Clinton remarked in response to the school killings in Littleton, Colorado, Americans must "do more to recognize the early warning signals" of how boys exhibit a capacity for violence (Kenworthy, 1999).

A New Vision:
Individuation and Connection
Do We Push Our Sons Away?

The cultural messages and cues that we parents have accepted as valid have their roots in traditional psychology. The traditional model of healthy adolescent development usually focuses on the task of separation and individuation, which is the process by which a person becomes a distinct individual. Accepted theory states that adolescents need to separate from both their parents' loving arms and their power (Gurian, 1996; Siegler, 1997; Erikson, 1963). In fact, in *Identity, Youth and Crisis,* Erik Erikson (1994) theorized that masculine identity is confirmed through separation, individuation, and autonomy. In *The Wonder of Boys,* Michael Gurian (1996) recommends that mothers give the following message to their sons: "Every day you need me less and less. And that's okay." It is commonly believed that even though separation is a painful and lonely transition, it's in the teenager's best interest. Indeed, Gurian (1996) blames mothers for giving the message, "I need you, don't go," which, he argues, creates an "adolescent entanglement" that makes it difficult for a boy to feel himself as real, whole, and capable of true commitment to mates.

This persistent and ubiquitous focus on separation has become the battle cry of traditional adolescent psychological theory. According to Ava Siegler's recent book, *The Essential Guide to the New Adolescence: How to Raise an Emotionally Healthy Teenager,* separation is a primary focus in a child's life from the time of his or her birth. From our focus groups, we found that mothers of boys often act from a frame

James is a night owl. He's a 16-year-old who goes to bed on school nights very late. While most of the evening he's involved with private activities like homework, using the computer, and telephoning, many nights at around 11:30 he becomes more animated and often bursts into our bedroom to alert us to Jerry Springer's outrageous talk show guest. To one program, his father's initial reaction was, "James, it's really late, and I prefer to watch the news and read before bedtime, especially when I have no interest in sensationalist television." However, my instinct was to respond differently to James's energy and desire to connect. While reiterating my distaste for the subject matter, I let him change the channel and discuss what he found so interesting. I understood that he was seeking our opinion and connecting to us by sharing his outrage. After the first time, my husband and I used this time as a way to discuss our values, even though the reason for or timing of the communication wasn't our choice. We met our son where he was, and didn't pass judgment on his interests. Instead, we reinforced his desire to come to us. —*Focus Group Mother*

of reference based on these traditional psychological theories and cultural experiences, and give their sons much more space than they give their daughters, almost tiptoeing around them. One mother reports, "My son likes to talk when he has a good day; when he is willing to talk, not when I want to talk." Another mother laments the fact that, "If he [her son] is in a bad mood, I stand back. Why should I feel like that?" A teacher told a story of working with boys in her photography class: "When the lights go out, they start to talk." It seems commonplace that our boys determine when they will talk and when they won't.

At the same time, these mothers find that their sons still need parenting, and, in fact, they worry about their sons confronting dangerous situations outside of the home. One mother recognizes that: "They [boys] see themselves as mature and responsible, but I see them as a target. But because my son is a boy and has a tough demeanor, I let him have more freedom than [I do] my daughter." These mothers echo our beliefs that they do not always have the necessary tools to parent their sons in ways that seem to work. Try this test to see what style of parent you are, so that you can begin to discover what tools you have to respond to your son's range of emotions.

PARENTING STYLES: A SELF TEST - WHAT STYLE OF PARENT ARE YOU?

For each item, please circle the choice that best fits how you feel.

1.   I think that anger is okay as long as it's under control.   T F
2.   A child's anger deserves a time-out.   T F
3.   When my child acts sad, he turns into a real brat.   T F
4.   When my child is sad, I am expected to fix the world and make it perfect.   T F
5.   If you ignore a child's sadness, it tends to go away and take care of itself.   T F
6.   Anger usually means aggression.   T F
7.   Sadness is something one has to get over, ride out, not dwell on.   T F
8.   When my child is sad, it's time to problem-solve.   T F
9.   I set limits on my child's anger.   T F
10. When my child acts sad, it's to get attention.   T F
11. Anger is an emotion worth exploring.   T F
12. I try to change my child's angry moods into cheerful ones.   T F
13. You should express the anger you feel.   T F
14. When my child is sad, it's a chance to get close.   T F
15. I want my child to experience sadness.   T F
16. The important thing is to find out why a child is feeling sad.   T F
17. When my child is sad, we sit down to talk about it.   T F
18. When my child is angry, it's an opportunity for getting close.   T F
19. The important thing is to find out why the child is feeling angry.   T F
20. If there is a lesson I have about sadness, it's that it's okay to express it.   T F
21. When my child is sad, I try to let him know that I love him, no matter what.   T F
22. When my child is sad, I'm not quite sure what he wants me to do.   T F
23. When my child is angry, I try to let him know that I love him, no matter what.   T F
24. When my child is angry, I'm not quite sure what he wants me to do.   T F
25. When my child gets angry, I worry about his destructive tendencies.   T F
26. Anger tends to cloud my judgment, and I do things I regret.   T F
27. When my child is angry, it's time to solve a problem.   T F
28. I don't make a big deal out of my child's anger.   T F
29. A child's anger is important.   T F
30. Children have a right to feel angry.   T F
31. When my child is mad, I try to find out what is making him mad.   T F
32. It's important to help the child find out what caused the child's anger.   T F
33. When my child gets angry with me, I think, "I don't want to hear this."   T F
34. When my child is angry, I think, "If only he could just learn to roll with the punches." T F
35. I want my child to get angry, to stand up for himself.   T F
36. When my child is angry, I want to know what he is thinking.   T F

FOUR STYLES OF PARENTING

HOW TO INTERPRET YOUR SCORES

The Terminator
Add up the number of times you said true for the following items:
1, 4, 5, 7, 12, 28, 33, 34

- wants the child's negative emotions to disappear quickly
- characteristically uses distraction to shut down the child's emotions
- may lack awareness of emotions in self and others
- feels uncomfortable, fearful, anxious, annoyed, hurt, or overwhelmed by the child's emotions

The Critic
Add up the number of times you said true for the following items:
2, 3, 6, 9, 10, 25, 26

- judges and criticizes the child's emotional expression
- reprimands, disciplines, or punishes the child for emotional expression, whether or not the child is misbehaving
- believes negative emotions reflect bad character traits

The Permissive
Add up the number of times you said true for the following items:
13, 20, 21, 22, 23, 24

- offers little guidance on behavior
- does not teach the child about emotions
- does not set limits

The Emotional Mentor
Add up the number of times you said true for the following items:
8, 11, 14, 15, 16, 17, 18, 19, 27, 29, 30, 31, 32, 35, 36

- values the child's negative emotions as an opportunity for intimacy
- can tolerate spending time with a sad, angry, or fearful child; does not become impatient with the emotion
- is aware of and values his or her own emotions

Now compare your four scores. The higher you scored in any one area, the more you tend toward that style of parenting. The lists shown summarize behaviors typical of each of four parenting styles.

EFFECTS OF THIS STYLE ON CHILDREN

- believes negative emotions are harmful or "will just make matters worse"
- minimizes the child's feelings, downplaying the events that led to the emotion
- doesn't problem-solve with the child

- They learn that their feelings are wrong, inappropriate, or invalid.
- They may learn that there is something inherently wrong with them because of the way they feel.
- They may have difficulty regulating and recognizing their own emotions.

- believes emotions make people weak, and children must be emotionally tough for survival
- believes negative emotions are unproductive, a waste of time

- Same as the terminator

- does not help children solve problems
- believes there is little one can do about negative emotions other than ride them out

- They don't learn to regulate their emotions.
- They have trouble concentrating, forming friendships, and getting along with other children.

- sees the world of negative emotions as an important area of parenting
- is sensitive to the child's emotional states, even when they are subtle
- does not tell the child how to feel
- does not feel he or she has to fix every problem for the child

- They learn to trust their feelings, regulate their own emotions, and solve problems.
- They have high self-esteem, learn well, and get along well with others.

Adapted with the permission of Simon and Schuster from *The Heart of Parenting: Raising an Emotionally Intelligent Child.* John Gottman and Jean DeClaire. ©1997 by John Gottman.

Your personal style of parenting greatly affects how you raise your son. Keep in mind that your parenting style is affected by your inherent emotional tendencies, all of the messages you are bombarded with from society, and your own childhood experiences.

With many experts warning mothers to let our sons separate, is it any wonder that we, as parents, feel pressured to push our boys away? In contrast, girls are expected to bond, despite research that demonstrates at birth that male babies are actually more expressive than female babies, and mothers tend to respond to their infant sons' negative states (eg., crying) less (Pollack, 1998). Feeling the need to separate from our sons begins almost at birth. One mother remembers how the day after her son was born she felt scared because he might be drafted one day. She recalls feeling the need to pull away from her baby even then to make him strong and protect him. Through many conversations with mothers, we found that the warnings from mental health professionals about the need for separation have become so ingrained in our popular culture that they make it appear to be dangerous for mothers even to express warmth to their sons, especially toward their adolescent sons. Some mothers can express love and warmth, but on a day-to-day basis may keep a hands-off approach so that, unlike their daughters, their sons are not expected to be emotionally responsible to the family. The common experience here is that mothers have enormous pressure on them to muffle their natural reactions to male children.

In focus groups and interviews, mothers confirmed this repeatedly. Mothers told us that they experience a unique self-consciousness with their sons that drives them to edit themselves for fear of "saying the

The path to becoming a better parent — like most every road to personal growth and mastery — begins with self-examination.

—John Gottman, The Heart of Parenting: Raising an Emotionally Intelligent Child

wrong thing." Rather than risk rebuke from their sons, mothers find themselves looking for information about their sons from others. As one mother stated when she was surprised to find out that her son had had a girlfriend for four months, "Information has to come in from the back door, and it takes a lot of energy to find the door."

Another mother recounted an experience that confirmed for her that she knows much less about her teenage son than she knew about her daughter at the same age. The mother explained that as homecoming weekend at her son's high school approached, she realized that she had no idea whether her son was going to attend the dance, whether he had a date, and, if he did, with whom. The night of the dance, this mother learned that, in fact, her son was going to the dance, with a date, and was also going to a dinner party that had been organized by several girls and their mothers. This mother reflected on the fact that, had it been her daughter's homecoming, she, as the mother, would have been highly involved with plans for the date and the dinner party. In another example of parents feeling left out of their son's lives, a mother reported that, as a last resort, she and her ex-husband have attempted to solve these types of problems with their son by holding weekly family meetings "to pull information" from him.

Fathers we spoke with also experienced this failure to "know." One father said, "I'm more careful about what I say. If he doesn't like what I'm saying, he shuts down the conversation." For example, his son may walk into a room, and when his dad tries to ask a question as benign as "How was your day?" or "Did you call your coach?" his son will lift his hand in a gesture that says, "Enough, I'm outta here." Another father concurred: "I understand her [his daughter] better than [I do] him. With my son, I wind up filling in a lot of blanks."

Each adolescent boy, and particularly older teens, feels he is expected to make his way in the world, almost without his parents' guidance. Many parents we spoke with, regardless of race, class, or ethnicity, talked about how they abdicate parenting their boys during adolescence. For example, parents reported that very few of them required their sons to inform them of their whereabouts on weekend evenings. In contrast, all of the parents of daughters required them to call if their plans changed during the course of an evening.

We believe that these differential expectations reflect the belief that if a boy doesn't separate from his mother, he will never achieve the independence necessary to discover his own psychological boundaries (Gurian, 1998). We believe that this model is too rigid and potentially dangerous. This socially supported separation is not always experienced as growth, but rather is an adaptation to a terrible loss (Betcher, 1995). This need for separation exerts tremendous power over the way we treat our sons to the exclusion of other factors.

The rationale behind this limiting, traditional model is that the separation will force the male teenager to rebuild his personality structure with minimal input from others, particularly adults. By developing a sense

Adolescents do not need separation from their parents, they need change in their relationship with their parents.... They need to preserve a deep underlying sense of connection with their parents.

—*Jean Baker Miller and Irene Stiver, Healing Connection: How Women Form Relationships in Therapy and in Life*

of himself independent from adults, a boy feels more competent. According to this model, parents' input is often thought to be emasculating, and to successfully complete his adolescent development, the boy needs to sever or loosen ties with his parents. It is not surprising that during this period, adolescent males often look to their peer group for support and guidance instead of their family.

On a brighter note, however, many respected, thoughtful professionals are finally turning their attention to this phase of boys' development, and have reframed the task so that "Adolescents do not need to separate from their parents, they need change in their relationship with their parents.... They need to preserve a deep underlying sense of connection with their parents" (Miller and Stiver, 1997). This new framework seems more realistic and compatible with our roles as mothers, fathers, and educators.

We have found that the way adolescent boys connect with others may be different from the way girls do. Connection for an adolescent boy may not be based on a deep, emotional exchange with another. In fact, connection with an adolescent boy may be difficult to even recognize at first because of its subtlety and possible contradiction of what we acknowledge as connection. In our focus groups, we learned that connection between a mother and son can take the form of a brief moment of agreement about an issue, an incident that reaffirms trust, or even an extended period of comfortable silence.

One mother told us the story of offering her son advice about a potential girlfriend. Her son was being pursued by a girl who had many boyfriends. The mother cautioned her son about the importance of making sure that he was not just another conquest. Weeks later, her son announced that he agreed with her advice, signaling to her that he had actively listened to her and valued her advice. Her son made this confession despite the fact that he had not even acknowledged the conversation.

Another mother related a simple verbal exchange with her son about how to handle his having missed a meeting scheduled with a teacher. Again, at the time her son did not respond to her advice. However, later, on the way to soccer practice, he told her that he knew she was always looking out for his best interests. Still another mother talked to us about taking an eight-hour car ride with her son in complete silence. She recognized that there was no need to force conversation. She recalled her own childhood and how comforting it had been to spend hours sitting next to her own father in total silence while they were fishing. She had followed her instincts, which told her that for her family, silence was okay.

In addition, another mother responded to this story stating that she had never understood what attracted boys and men to fishing until she looked at her son at camp as he was fishing with other boys on the edge of the lake. She realized that the silence of fishing was a bonding experience and a moment for connection. Perhaps our very concept of what it means to be connected is based on a female model that needs to be adjusted to meet males' different needs.

Chapter 3

New Challenges for Building Connections
What Can We Do to Foster Closeness?

We have found that much of contemporary psychological theory and many therapeutic approaches are based on the fear of children becoming dependent and enmeshed. Becoming a man is understood as becoming autonomous, self-sufficient, independent, and, of course, separate. This may be achieved at the expense of learning how to stay connected with others, be intimate, have family responsibilities, and create a community. We support the biological and psychological hard data that demonstrate the benefits of what has been called a "sponsored independence," abandoning the artificial choice currently offered to our boys of distancing themselves from their parents or feeling too involved with them (Adams, 1998). We believe "real freedom comes from choosing interdependence rather than the false choice between co-dependence and independence…the capacity for love and intimacy — an open heart — is so important to having a joyful life as well as to survival" (Ornish, 1997).

As parents, we need to understand that adolescent boys still need adult guidance and support. It is this guidance that makes a boy feel that he is working with a "safety net," while he begins to experiment with his own independence. We need to have confidence in our own ability to provide that safety net, regardless of our marital status, socioeconomic background, or ethnicity. It is important that our boys understand that they are not alone; we are there to guide them toward independence.

Too many parents allow their sons to move into the world without really letting their sons know that they will function as their sons' safety net. Part of this process of connecting is to teach boys that there is no shame in needing or using this net. Just as a child learns to walk one step at a time, a boy should learn to become a man, building connections and independence as he grows. The notion of separation as the main goal of a successful adolescence completely dismisses the psychological theories of attachment and the research that shows that connection is a more valuable goal (Bowlby, 1980). Boys traditionally become men in our society by learning to fear entanglement and emasculation. Thus, boys may satisfy their need for connectedness in positive and negative ways, such as joining a sports team or joining a gang.

Underneath it all there is a desperate need to connect. —Annette Bening discussing her film, American Beauty

While we are pushing boys away, connection does remain significant to them. Within our focus groups, and in our own personal experiences, we have listened to boys talk about their need to connect with others. An overriding theme for these boys is the importance of loyalty among their peers. In this context, many boys speak of peer friendships, with girls and boys, as one of the most important aspects of their lives. Loyalty among friends is more important than participating in sports together, enjoying the same music, or "hanging out" together. One boy said, "A true friend is someone who, when the drama comes, doesn't run." We're all aware that teenagers spend a majority of their time with their peers in school, in after-school and weekend activities, and, for what seems an eternity, on the telephone. Through these activities, adolescent boys are constantly developing, maintaining, and learning about connections with others. This potentially positive side of peer relations is rarely talked about or acknowledged by adults. However, the acts of violence that we are witnessing in our schools show the dark side of failed peer relationships and the absence of a society that sanctions an adult safety net for boys (Murray, 1999).

The relationships that boys develop take on different forms. We found in our focus groups that boys may connect with some of their friends in a way that is different from how girls connect with their friends. All of the boys in our groups talked about the importance of friendship between boys, and they spoke a good deal about "joking around" together.

However, the boys seem to have a set of implicit rules about this joking. They talked about setting clear subject matter and interpersonal boundaries, such as issues around family. For example, some words are okay to use among close friends, whereas in other contexts they might precipitate a fight. It appears that for boys, joking is a way of expressing intimacy among male friends.

Boys express intimacy in other ways as well. We have found that boys tend to form relationships with other boys based on their participation in similar activities that may or may not require substantive verbal communication. Some of the boys acknowledged having close male friends with whom they talked about "things." While writing this book, one of our sons asked the question, "What do you think we talk about? You think that all we talk about is sports and girls. We talk 5 percent about school, 10 percent about sports, 40 percent about girls, and the other 45 percent about life." One mother told us how her son and his friends rallied around a friend whose father had died suddenly. All of the boys supported each other and dropped everything else they were doing to be there for this boy. It was obvious that the boys genuinely

As the New York Yankees celebrated their latest World Series championship victory with the customary bear hugs, high fives, and champagne, millions of Americans also saw most of these young men, all of whom embody our ultimate masculine ideal, shed real tears while they hugged each other and comforted teammates who had experienced loss and tragedy throughout the season. Beyond the typical team camaraderie, these men felt extremely connected in ways that were more about their collective humanity than about wins and losses. Watching the players connect to each other demonstrated the capacity of men and boys to comfort each other. After the stunning victory, the Yankees manager, Joe Torre, said, "I'll tell you, during my tough time this spring, I showed up at hospitals for different scans and different stuff, and George Steinbrenner was there all the time. So we have this closeness right now. I enjoy it. He does. And to make it even better, we've been successful doing it." —*Erik Brady, "Cancer Gave Torre New Outlook on the Game"*

AS THE NEW YORK YANKEES CELEBRATED...

connected emotionally around this issue. These particular boys "took care of each other" by calling each other, keeping friends informed, and encouraging other friends to reach out to the boy when a friend was less inclined to do that.

Nearly all of the boys interviewed stated that they also had at least one close female friend with whom they talked. The boys went so far as to tell us that if they were on the phone after 10 p.m., it was surely with a girl.

At the same time, boys expressed a great deal of loyalty to their families, citing insults to family members as one of the most disrespectful comments they could receive. All of the boys who were relatively successful in school mentioned at least one adult whom they trusted and with whom they had a good relationship, whether it was an older sibling, family friend, grandparent, teacher, aunt or uncle, or parent. The more boys were disengaged from school the less likely they were to be attached to their family or some significant adult. We found in our conversations

with boys that while autonomy is extremely important for them, they don't want it at the expense of losing closeness with others. Many mothers talked about the closeness their sons had with extended family members. One mother said, "Even when my son refuses to go out to dinner with us, he never misses a chance to spend time with his cousins." Those who didn't have that closeness were more likely to replace it with the contemporary "family" of an organized gang or other antisocial relationships.

Even Albert Einstein provides insight into the ways in which separateness can lead to alienation and violence when he talks about "falling into the delusion of separateness." Dean Ornish (1997) reports that in response to a letter written by a rabbi who was grieving over the death of his daughter, Einstein wrote that "separation is an optical illusion of consciousness, and that if we see things only in that framework, we become locked in a prison and lose the capacity to be intimate, compassionate, to know ourselves in the larger sense." The real challenge is to give boys opportunities to be independent and autonomous, without being disconnected. One mother recounted a related incident about her teenage son. When her son's religious school was taking a trip to New York City, the children were heavily scheduled for most of the day. However, her son had extended family in New York, and one cousin had just given birth to a baby. He expressed a strong interest in seeing the baby, which reminded his parents how important it was for him to be connected to his family. His parents supported their son's feelings and made arrangements for him to see the baby.

The role of the family as the primary form of connection is well described in the popular book, *Tuesdays with Morrie*. When facing his death, Morrie Schwartz tells his former student, Mitch Albom, the most important lesson that he has learned in his life. Morrie says, "Invest in the human family. Invest in people. Build a little community of those you love and who love you. In the beginning of life, when we are infants, we need others to survive, right? And at the end of life, when you get like me, you need others to survive, right? But here's the secret; in between, we need others as well" (Albom, 1997).

FAMILY MESSAGES

We all carry family messages with us that help to form our values. When you were growing up, what messages or information did you receive from your mother and other adult women about the importance of the following:

Success in school?

Appearance?

Using drugs or alcohol?

Having sex?

Marriage?

Career?

Children?

When you were growing up, what messages or information did you receive from your father and other adult men about the importance of the following:

Success in school?

Appearance?

Using drugs or alcohol?

Having sex?

Marriage ?

Career ?

Children?

What messages will you or do you tell your children or students about the importance of the following:

Success in school?

Appearance?

Using drugs or alcohol ?

Having sex?

Marriage?

Career?

Children?

The answers to these questions help to provide insight, not only into what you say, but how you communicate messages to your sons. This insight is necessary to strengthen connections between parents and sons.

Parents often don't recognize the significance of boys connecting and supporting each other. One mother in our focus group shared her recognition of how boys connect during sad and challenging times. She described seeing her son greet his closest friend by tapping him on the back as he was getting into the car to attend a funeral of a friend's father. They didn't speak, they didn't have to, because the communication and support was obvious without words. Soon after the sudden death of a close peer in a car accident, two teenage boys asked one of their mothers to drive them to their late friend's home. They wanted to tell the parents how much they would miss their friend (Britt, 1998). These are the kinds of cues that we need to watch for and nourish in our sons.

In response to this incident, we can't help asking the following questions: What are the feelings of our boys who live in neighborhoods where death of their peers is an everyday occurrence? What are we doing to help these boys channel their fears and sorrows in directions that are not violent? As parents, we need to provide our sons with the skills they need to connect with their feelings and channel their anger into productive alternatives. With these skills, boys will feel less fearful of and more competent in connecting.

Much of contemporary parenting inadvertently inhibits and stunts the emotional growth of boys. For the last 30 years, we've expanded the opportunities for girls; the time has come to refocus our attention on the emotional needs of boys. Meeting this challenge will enhance the emotional well-being of all our children. The boys we interviewed feel pressure "to be stronger." Many admit that "there is a lot of stress being a boy," and they grow into men sorting out life's challenges without knowing how to ask for help. The following rap lyrics express one boy's frustrations and his desire to find tranquility.

I've got to sort

to find a way to be

inbounds when I play on the

court, but I got no traction

so I'm tripping, tripping, not living

positive, so I am asking

but I feel that I'm taunted

in some kind of noose that became

haunted, by ghosts and evils and

America's Most Wanted,

I don't know where to

look or to find the answer,

this thing is evil, starts small

and if not found early is like

cancer, it spreads and beheads

even the MC breakdancer

— Teddy Sczudlo

Lyrics used with permission of Teddy Sczudlo. ©2000.

These lyrics are an example of the introspection and sensitivity boys can feel, although they don't always display such emotions on the surface or in ways that parents easily understand. Since boys' emotions tend to remain hidden, we must be ready to look at all outlets of expression to discover what our boys are feeling.

Again, as Morrie Schwartz recognized, "The fact is, there is no foundation, no secure ground, upon which people may stand today if it isn't the family. It's become quite clear to me as I've been sick. If you don't have the support and love and caring and concern that you get from a family, you don't have much at all. Love is so supremely important. As our great poet Auden said, 'Love each other or perish'" (Albom, 1997). From another perspective, Marian Wright Edelman (1996) writes, "I urge every parent and adult to conduct a personal audit to determine whether we are contributing to the crisis our children face or to the solutions they urgently need. Our children don't need or expect us to be perfect. They do need and expect us to be honest, to admit and correct our mistakes, and to share our struggles about the meanings and responsibilities of faith, parenthood, citizenship and life." Parents should not apologize for teaching their teenage sons about the importance of ethics and commitment to family. We should feel confident because we are making the family a priority.

The Veil of Masculinity
What Is the Impact of "Boys Will Be Boys"?

The crisis among American boys is different, but no less serious, from that of their sisters. Our experience shows us, and research supports the notion, that we treat our sons differently from our daughters. The majority of the boys with whom we spoke agreed that they are treated differently by their parents and other adults because they are boys. For example, we give our boys more freedom than we give our girls. One girl remarked, "If you are a girl, your parents will be much more protective of you. My parents have a lot of trouble with my growing up and being more independent." A *Newsweek* story, "Guns and Dolls," quoted psychology professor Carol Z. Malatesta, who found that mothers displayed a wider range of emotional responses to girls than to boys (Shapiro, 1998). Other researchers found that mothers talk about emotions in different ways with their daughters from the way they do with their sons (Fivush, 1989; Levant, 1995). They talk more about feelings, like crying, with their daughters, and talk more about negative emotions, like anger, with their sons.

In the same article, Judith Smetana, associate professor of pediatrics at the University of Rochester, found that mothers were more likely to deal differently with misbehavior, depending on the child's gender. Boys were punished more than girls, and girls were interrupted more frequently by their parents. Some boys also said that their parents seemed more suspicious of their conduct, often assuming they were misbehaving without trying to learn the full story. One mother confirmed this perception: "When I see my son in trouble, to me it would be trouble that he caused." At home, and in school, boys experience this differential treatment based on their gender.

Boys in our focus groups reported how they were treated differently from their sisters. As one boy observed, "When they [sisters] give them that sweet face, they can get what they're asking for." According to these boys, their parents, "Let her [the sister] do what she wants," "They always tell me no and they tell her yeah," and "They give her what she wants when she asks for it." Although it's hard to admit, we parents expect our sons to solve problems for themselves, but readily jump in to protect our daughters by trying to solve their problems for them.

DIFFERENTIAL TREATMENT ON THE BASIS OF GENDER

Take a few minutes to answer these questions:

1. Do you treat your children of different sexes differently from one another? If so, how?

2. Do you have a stronger relationship with one child than another? If so, why?

Now ask your children their opinions:

1. Are you treated differently from your brother or sister? If so, how?

2. Do you have a stronger relationship with one parent than the other? If so, why?

3. Is there anyone you wish to be like in your family?

4. What do your parents expect for your future?

   Do they expect the same things for your brother or sister?

After completing this quiz and hearing your children's opinions, take some time to think about the similarities and differences in your responses and the impact of sex roles on family life.

One area in which we treat our sons and daughters differently concerns physical affection. Many parents remember the moment when their little boy began to stiffen when hugged or kissed in public. In a focus group, one mother recalled this turning point with her son; when he turned 12, he said to her, "I just can't hug you now. I know I will again one day." As early as the age of five, boys begin announcing to parents that kisses are no longer acceptable. One mother tells us about saying good-bye to her son. When she carpools her nine-year-old son and his friends to school, he waits for his friends to walk away from the car and then comes around to the driver's side to kiss his mother good-bye. Hugging and kissing is a normal part of greeting and expressing love and friendship between men and between parents and children in other cultures. The restraints boys feel on these types of affection in American culture cannot be blamed on biology.

In addition to trying to cope with a double standard for their conduct, boys are bombarded with conflicting messages about men and masculinity. On the one hand, society tells boys that men are cool, confident, and always in control. On the other hand, boys and men are told to be sensitive and not hide their feelings. At the same time, they are also expected to hide any "feminine" emotions for fear of being labeled a "wuss." This fear is evident in the ways boys talk about homosexuality. The conflicting messages about desirable conduct cause great confusion for boys.

David Dyson/Camera Press/Retna

The first publicized kiss between Prince William and Prince Charles in August, 1998.

In one of our focus groups, the boys from all ethnicities agreed that they don't speak to other boys on the telephone late at night because of the level of intimacy implied in a late-night conversation. In another group, some boys said that they cannot accept homosexuals, others said that

Michael Thompson *(Protecting the Emotional Life of Boys)* says, "Boys enforce a view of masculinity on each other. If you show anything too tender, feminine, compassionate, empathetic, you're a wuss, you're gay. At some point early on, boys begin to measure everything they do on one level: strong or weak."

—*Joan Ryan, "Boys to Men"*

although they can accept homosexuality as a valid sexual orientation, they prefer not to spend much time with overtly "feminine" boys for fear of such boys "coming on" to them. Some girls in our focus groups confirmed this self-consciousness. One girl told us that when boys participate in traditionally feminine activities, such as dance and drama, they risk being labeled gay. The pressure not to disclose sexual preference makes many gay and bisexual teens more likely to attempt suicide and take risks, sexual and otherwise, that endanger their health (Nightline, 1999).

Another target of attack is a boy's competence. Boys' fear of failure and discomfort with intimacy also comes from needing to avoid being labeled a "wuss," "pansy," "fag," "loser," "dork," or "mama's boy," and from needing others to affirm his competence. According to the American Association of University Women (AAUW) report *Hostile Hallways,* 85 percent of the boys surveyed agreed that being called any name that is related to being gay is the worst possible insult. This is confirmed by later surveys of thousands of adolescent boys on issues related to sexual harassment; they too reported their fear of the stigma of being called gay (American Association of University Women, 1998).

In today's schools, students think there is nothing more demeaning than to be called gay; anti-gay harassment is not just directed at gays and lesbians, it's the most common form of harassment. — Rebecca Jones, "I Don't Feel Safe Here Anymore: Your Legal Duty to Protect Gay Kids from Harassment"

To hide any appearance of having "soft" emotions, boys create a shield, like armor, to protect themselves. This shield takes the form of maintaining a veil of apparent competence, which makes it difficult for boys to communicate freely about fears or feelings or even to ask for help. For instance, working with our focus groups, we found that boys chose their words extremely carefully. They also looked for indirect cues from the group about when and how to respond to questions.

When asked to talk about themselves, boys frequently did two things. First, they defined themselves, not by stating what they were, but rather how they were different from others (usually girls) in the group. For example, "Boys aren't…." rather than "Boys are…." Second, boys often referred to themselves in either the second person, "you," or the first person, plural, "we." Rarely did boys use the singular first person, "I." These patterns of speech may suggest a reluctance on the part of boys to talk in a personal, intimate way.

Boys will connect when they are not threatened, however. While boys often employ language shields, the girls with whom we spoke told us that boys can overcome them. The girls told us that in their one-on-one friendships with boys, they are able to communicate openly. One girl reported, "I have a really, really good guy friend. I tell him maybe more than I tell my girlfriends. And he shares everything with me, even emotions. I also find that I can do anything in front of him, and I feel comfortable around him." Even though boys may find occasional safe outlets for their emotions and behaviors, their shield is the primary image they show to the outside world. This is usually expressed with the ever-present: "No problem," "Don't sweat it," "Don't worry about it," "I can handle it," all expressions of manufactured self-confidence and bravado. We have provided the following checklist to help you assess your teenage son for potential problems.

> **Black and Hispanic boys can experience particular problems in adolescence, researchers say, because when they act peer-pleasingly tough, adults see them as dangerous and threatening, but if they act soft, they are likelier to be victimized.**
> —*William Pollack, "Real Boys: Rescuing Our Sons from the Myths of Boyhood"*

Does your teenager exhibit:	Regularly	Occasionally	Never
Social disconnection	○	○	○
Withdrawal	○	○	○
Masked emotions	○	○	○
Silence	○	○	○
Rage	○	○	○
Trouble with friends	○	○	○
Hypervigilence	○	○	○
Cruelty towards children/animals	○	○	○
Excessive interest in violent media	○	○	○
Unusual interest in weapons	○	○	○
Fascination with violent Internet sites	○	○	○
Interest in bombs, explosives	○	○	○
Excessive time spent playing violent video games	○	○	○

SHOULD YOU WORRY ABOUT YOUR SON?

If you are at all concerned, check out your observations with another adult and/or a mental health professional. Don't dismiss what you see. We need to call attention to the dangers inherent in "shrugging off" inappropriate behavior.

The "boys will be boys" response may result in excessively aggressive behavior, such as sexual harassment and bullying. The generally accepted notion of this "natural boyish" behavior has long allowed sexual harassment and bullying to be dismissed as an unfortunate, yet unavoidable part of experiencing adolescence when, in reality, these are serious offenses that affect students' self-esteem and readiness to learn. As a result, many students feel victimized, degraded, fearful, uncomfortable, and rejected. The statistics on sexual harassment and bullying in school speak to the scope of the problem:

- Eighty-one percent of students surveyed in 8th through 11th grades experienced some form of sexual harassment (American Association of University Women, 1998).

- Seventy-six percent of boys report being targets of harassment in school. In particular, the rates for African American boys are higher than for Whites or Latinos. This harassment most commonly takes the form of sexual comments, jokes, gestures, or looks, with sexual touching and grabbing being the second most common type. Boys are most frequently harassed in enclosed areas such as locker rooms and restrooms, by both girls and boys, and in general are less likely than girls to report such incidents (American Association of University Women, 1993).

- Four out of five Seattle students who had experienced antigay harassment said they were actually heterosexual. Those children were three times as likely as their nonharassed heterosexual peers to have missed at least one day of school in the previous month because of fear for their safety (Jones, 1999).

- Boys report a slightly higher rate of experience as perpetrators of harassment: two-thirds of all boys and more than half of the girls surveyed admitted that they have sexually harassed someone in school (American Association of University Women, 1998).

Teachers, coaches, and school administrators often do little to stop sexual harassment and bullying, frequently acting as disinterested bystanders while students are harassed and bullied in their presence. When school staff members do step in, they tend to do so privately, on a case-by-case basis. They do not follow up by using these incidents to change or initiate new school policy, raise awareness, or institute preventive training on the issue (Phillips, 1998). However, one study discovered that those schools with strong sexual harassment policies took action against an alleged harasser 84 percent of the time (Smith, 1998).

Furthermore, when sexual harassment policies do exist, the grievance procedures that are in place, along with the training of staff and students, are frequently implemented ineffectively. The existing training appears to place all the responsibility on the girls, teaching them to say "no," rather than training both boys and girls to behave respectfully toward one another (Phillips, 1998).

In the face of these statistics, parents may want some insight into why this behavior is an acceptable part of "Boys will be boys." They may want to ask themselves: Are boys cut loose from parental influence too early? Cate Dooley, co-director of the Mother-Son Project at Wellesley College in Wellesley, Massachusetts, states: "Any parent can testify that boys are subject to a much earlier, more abrupt campaign to extinguish the compassion, empathy, and expression of feeling that young boys display as openly as girls" (Coontz, 1997). So, by believing the myth that all adolescent boys must exhibit some form of aggressive behavior as an essential part of their development, parents may be neglecting the difficult task of understanding how these issues apply to their individual sons, and what their role should be in addressing these issues.

The seductiveness of this abdication can be understood more fully when considered in light of the shield that boys wear, and the battles parents must engage in with their sons when trying to get close to them. One mother told us, "It seems that boys feel if they are too close, or give too much information, they are giving up power." The boys in our focus groups confirmed this observation when some revealed that they were fully aware of their efforts to keep their parents at a distance, in part by offering a minimal amount of information about their lives. A father clearly conceded his abdication: "If I give him freedom, independence, and privacy, we have more of a chance of having a relationship."

What does it cost boys to give up traditional expectations about their masculinity? If the boys in your life don't fit the "ideal male" image, descriptions of these behaviors question their masculinity. For example, the list of derogatory words for a boy who acts feminine is much longer than the list of negative words for a girl who acts masculine. The consequence is that boys may feel embarrassed for showing any soft or emotional attributes or behaviors, including intimacy.

To think about your perspective on traditional expectations for boys, complete the following exercise. Jot down some of the adjectives you use to describe the ideal man and woman. Refer to the following attributes, or come up with others that describe your personal views:

ZITS   **BY JERRY SCOTT AND JIM BORGMAN**

Reprinted with special permission of King Features Syndicate.

affectionate, willing to take risks, aggressive, acts as a leader, cheerful, forceful, competitive, sympathetic, loyal, loves children, self-reliant, domineering, ambitious, childlike, athletic, understanding, yielding, willing to take a stand, strong personality, tender, soft-spoken, shy, self-sufficient, gentle, sensitive to the needs of others, does not use harsh language, assertive, eager to soothe hurt feelings, able to analyze a situation, independent, individualistic, makes decisions easily, good with machines, defends own beliefs, compassionate, very concerned with appearance.

Your Ideal Man and Woman

Ideal Man	Ideal Woman
1.	
2.	
3.	
4.	
5.	

After composing your lists, consider your opinions regarding gender. Do you have two very different lists, with certain qualities you label feminine and others masculine? Or are the lists similar, and made up of qualities you feel are important regardless of gender? Are there any qualities that you consider positive if exhibited by one gender, but find negative when exhibited in the opposite gender (e.g., some people want to see aggression in males but dislike an aggressive female)? Do you feel your opinions are similar to those of society in general? By examining your opinions and recognizing typical gender stereotypes, you'll be able to better understand the choices presented to boys.

One often hears in our society, "If his father had been a different sort of man, then his problems would have been quite different." But it would be even truer to comment also: "If he had been born into a society with a different form of fatherhood...." —*Margaret Mead, Male and Female: The Classic Study of the Sexes*

The consequences of repressed feelings? Emotionally empty relationships. Ulcers. Risky behavior. Whereas girls might turn to starvation or self-mutilation as emotional outlets, boys might drive too fast, drink too much, take drugs, commit vandalism, skip school, and sleep around. The girls' behavior is seen as self-destructive and a plea for help, the boys' behavior is often dismissed as simply "bad." —*Joan Ryan, "Boys to Men"*

The necessary process of proving one's masculinity can become a socially mandated burden. Boys are expected to restrict their displays of affection by maintaining their shield of competence. We expect boys to be tough, independent, and autonomous (Real, 1997). Society teaches us that boys and men are less in need of friends, close bonds, connections, and intimacy. For boys, success in adulthood has little to do with relationships. They place less value on being successful husbands or fathers. This expectation is reserved for girls and women, and becomes their lifelong responsibility.

One story we heard bears repeating. Several of the boys in one of our focus groups experienced Morrie Schwartz's teachings, as described in *Tuesdays with Morrie,* firsthand, when a friend's father died quite unexpectedly. The boys responded by calling their friend continuously and offering support. One of the boys reported that he was surprised that so many school friends were unsure about calling the grieving friend. The friends closest to the boy whose father had died found themselves assuring the others that it was more important to reach out and call him than to worry about appearing foolish. From this experience, some of the boys learned about the importance of community during times of sorrow. The boys' hesitancy to act on their feelings is not surprising, since society tends to frown on males' public display of affection and empathy. It is important to note here that the parents of these boys who reached out to their friend encouraged this display of empathy and caring.

Living in a culture that doesn't support boys' emotional expression puts pressure on them not to talk. As a result, one father told us, "I feel like I'm Sherlock Holmes trying to find information [about my son]." Another father lamented, "I feel I can't get to his core, we can't deal with big issues." Boys begin to feel that to be masculine, they have to deal with everything themselves. A girl in one of our focus groups said it best: "Telling your parents things helps them to see that you're growing up. Boys shut parents out to tell them that they're growing up."

This tendency of boys to shut down verbally is also present in school. Girls notice that, in school, "We can tell people what we think about things. Boys are not as sure of themselves to say something." Another girl remarked, "My English teacher is always yelling at guys. I talk just as much, if not more, but my teacher expects that I always have something thoughtful to say." Although research does show that boys are called on to answer questions more than girls, several boys reported that they also are expected to act out and not be "as mature as girls" (American Association of University Women, 1998; Sadker and Sadker, 1994).

As parents and educators, we know that subscribing to a narrow definition of "boys will be boys," puts limits on the development of our sons and can be a self-fulfilling prophecy. As one veteran teacher said,

Boys in our focus groups reported that teachers "tend to be more easy on girls." For example, Sam experienced this reaction to handing in his homework late: "Like with homework, like if you didn't do your homework and you ask to turn it in the next day, they might say no to you and yes to a girl. I've seen that happen." — *Focus Group Boy*

When we ask the master teacher, the veteran who is helping the student teacher, about the boys in his class, he pulls no punches: "They're sloppy, noisy, immature. I don't know the reason, but, compared to boys, the girls are a pleasure to teach. Actually, these boys are not bad. When I was teaching in Baltimore, we were warned about being hit or shot. Here the boys are difficult but not dangerous. We just try to keep them calm and working." — *High School Teacher*

"What you expect, you get!" After being in the classroom for 30 years, he acknowledges that when he looks at his biases, he realizes he assumes that girls are more conscientious in class, more mature, and more serious about their studies than boys. These kinds of rigid assumptions are detrimental to our sons. We have a responsibility to look beyond the stereotypes associated with gender in the most subtle and obvious areas, including our families, schools, and culture; in the language we use; and in our expectations of how we define a "normal" boy and a "normal" girl. The conditions we discuss in the next chapter offer some examples of the impact of "Boys will be boys."

What Statistics Tell Us
What Is It Really Like to Be a Boy Today?

Conditions for boys growing up today are not as favorable as many believe. A myth about boys would have us believe that boys "have it easy," and success comes effortlessly to them. Moreover, they are independent, confident, and need little help. In fact, this myth has perpetuated the rigid models for raising and connecting with boys, described earlier, and has had a profound impact on boys.

Parents and teachers have applied these myths with devastating consequences. The image of the male as strong is confused with the image of the male as aggressive and violent. Virility has been replaced with promiscuity. Adventurousness has evolved into recklessness. Intelligence often is confused with bravado and arrogance. In the following pages, we debunk the myth that boys have it easy using research-based evidence. We discuss differences between boys and girls as well as differences among boys.

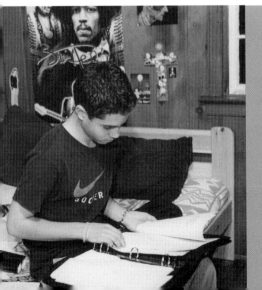

Eighth-grade boys are 50 percent more likely than girls to be held back a grade. Boys are more likely to drop out of high school than girls. Boys are three times more likely to be victims of violence. Adolescent boys commit most of the adolescent crimes. What is happening to our boys?
— *Montgomery County Youth Workers Training Committee, "Young and Male: How to Nurture Adolescent Boys into Loving and Responsible Men"*

Education

While this myth would have us believe that boys naturally excel in school, the facts show that many boys experience clear signs of educational failure. Boys, particularly boys of color, drop out of school at much higher rates than girls. More boys are identified for special education programs than girls. Boys are more likely to fail a course or be retained at grade level. Boys are more likely to experience discipline problems in school. And boys score much lower than girls on reading and writing skills tests. For educators, these findings raise a fundamental question about our attitudes toward boys' academic performance: Is their poor performance a question of maturity, that "boys will be boys," and then they'll catch up later? Or do boys genuinely underperform? If so, should we rethink how they are raised and educated?

> On back-to-school night, one high school teacher said in response to a parent who worried that her daughter was quiet in class, "Don't worry, the boys make all the noise and the girls get A's." —*High School Teacher*

Academic Environment

Considering the role schools play in the lives of boys, it's important to examine what impact they are having on boys today. In addition to providing knowledge and skills, the school environment and curriculum significantly influence boys' socialization, from the ages of five to 18. During these years, boys spend the majority of their time in school, academic courses, and extracurricular activities, such as school athletics.

Schools begin causing boys stress in the early years of elementary school. The school environment is not structured for boys' energy or motor skill development. Boys and girls develop at different rates physically and intellectually. Boys are thrown into the school environment, where they may not perform well initially. Girls read faster and pay attention better. Boys are physically more restless and impulsive. When boys enter school at the age of five or six, their motor skills — such as the ability to hold a pencil — are usually less developed than those of girls (Kantrowitz and Kalb, 1998).

Reading is a critical factor in boys' difficulties in school. Adolescent boys are, on average, 18 months behind their female peers in reading and writing (Henderson, 1999). Within many families, this may be because reading is perceived as a female activity, even though it's fundamental to academic progress. Rough and tumble activities are seen as the preserve of boys. As one elementary teacher observed, "Girls have a realistic expectation of what school is like and are more likely than boys to be ready to sit still and listen." Young boys tend to be more active than girls, and in the school environment this is looked on as bad behavior. The result is that young boys begin to experience frustration with their academic abilities and self-esteem very early on (Kantrowitz and Kalb, 1998). These issues are more complex when diverse cultures are introduced into the equation. African American and Latino boys raised in expressive cultures may have the most difficulty with the more traditionally passive, quiet, European American models common in most schools (Murray, 1999).

Choices become increasingly limited for boys as they progress through school. By the time children enter middle school, gender stereotyping is predominant. When we asked boys in our focus groups, "Do you think people treat you differently in school because you are a boy?" the majority responded with a resounding yes! Teachers and administrators come to expect certain behaviors from boys, such as aggressiveness and social immaturity. Teachers may actually expect disruptive and antisocial behavior from boys of color. They respond to their beliefs about and fears of such behavior by restricting boys to traditional male values of competition and hierarchy (Pollack, 1998; Thompson, 1988; Smith, 1994).

In fact, Samuel Shem and Janet Surrey (1998) argue that, while elementary school staffs often praise students for "working well with others and helping others work," this characteristic is rarely recognized or rewarded in middle and high schools. According to psychologist Michael Thompson (1999), "We sometimes don't make accommodations for the boys' developmental levels, so we humiliate them and get them mad, or interpret their activity as willful aggression, and so begins the fulfillment of a prophecy where we try to punish and control boys more harshly than girls, and they come to resent and dislike it, and dislike authority, and react back against it."

Among students, it is accepted that boys tend to receive harsher punishment than girls for similar infractions. For example, in one of our focus groups, a teenage girl explained that she comes to one particular class consistently late, but is simply given a verbal reminder to be on time. In contrast, she has noticed that when boys are late to the same class, they are removed from the classroom. Another teenage girl told of a similar experience. She noticed at her school that girls often get away with walking freely down the hall when it's obvious they don't have a hall pass. Again, in contrast, she has seen boys stopped and questioned, even when they were openly displaying their hall passes. Students also reported that Latino and African American males were the most likely to be severely reprimanded or harassed by teachers.

Still another story illustrates this point. One of our peer groups was made up of a group of teenage boys from the same large urban high school. They told us that some of the boys' bathrooms in their school were locked, ostensibly to prevent loitering. In contrast, all of the girls' bathrooms were open all of the time. The boys blamed their treatment on stereotypes about their behavior, citing a recent discipline problem in one open girls' bathroom. Such "inflexible codes" in schools guide boys into strictly defined roles (Sadker and Sadker, 1994).

Even courses of study and extracurricular activities in a school can reinforce the "inflexible code" that we impose upon boys. For instance, students are exposed to few examples of nontraditional male role models

> Scenes like this one are played out daily in schools across America: Two seniors, Kyle and Michelle, arrive at their high school English class 15 minutes late. The teacher stares at them as they enter the room. "Kyle, do you need a special invitation? Is it too much to ask that you get here on time? Never mind. Sit down and see me after class. [Pause; voice softens.] And, Michelle, I'm disappointed in you."
> — *Two High School Students*

in the classroom and in the curriculum they study. Most history curriculum is filled with the achievements of a few famous White men who have succeeded through "typical" male behaviors (Smith, 1994; Thompson, 1988). This lack of exposure to a wider variety of male role models can have the effect of limiting boys' choices, career options, and plans for the future. For boys of color, this problem is magnified by the fact that most textbooks contain very few examples of African American, Latino, or Asian men (or women) who have successfully contributed to our community and/or national history.

In a review of the most widely used high school health education textbooks, we found that sex role stereotypes are prevalent. Females are still pictured in discussions and illustrations related to nutrition, childcare, psychological aspects of love and caring, and personal care related to physical appearance. Male models are virtually never pictured as caregivers, and appear only in discussions of competition, violence, stress, and mental disorders. When individuals are pictured in their jobs, women are shown as nurses, mothers, and one doctor, while men are shown as welders, athletes, doctors, farmers, police officers, broadcasters, and architects (Shaffer and Shevitz, 1999). These texts fail our children by continuing to portray groups in stereotypical or narrowly defined ways, virtually ignoring the wide range of individual interests and abilities within any such group. More important, believing in these

One star athlete recalled his pre- and post-star treatment by his teachers. After several football victories, he said, "I'm now getting the attention from my teachers that I always wanted."

—*Focus Group Boy*

stereotypes virtually prevents boys from considering the benefits of seeking careers that either require or allow them to express their feelings.

The "inflexible code" also steers most boys into a narrow range of after-school activities.As we said earlier, more than three times as many boys spend their extracurricular time involved in team sports than in any other type of school activity (U.S. Department of Education, 1996b). Our focus groups with boys and girls confirmed this statistic. When asked what clubs or activities they participate in, the boys overwhelmingly listed various team sports. Only very few of the boys listed other clubs, such as ethnic-affiliation clubs. When asked why they didn't participate in a greater variety of activities, the boys seemed to believe that sports were a societal priority they were expected to do. One boy talked about how his teachers rewarded his participation on a varsity sports team: "Some teachers are more lenient with male athletes; they let them get away with more." Several mothers of boys in one of our focus groups said that boys will only participate in an activity outside of this "inflexible code" under unusual circumstances, such as in a non-traditional, smaller school environment.

On the other hand, girls are one and a half times more likely than boys to participate in non-athletic school activities, including student government; academic honor society; yearbook/newspaper; school service clubs; school hobby clubs; and Future Teachers of America, Future Homemakers of America, and Future Farmers of America (U.S. Department of Education, 1996b). Again, our conversations with girls confirm this. In our focus groups, girls cited a wide range of activities in which they participate, including, but not dominated by, team sports.

Unlike boys, girls don't feel constrained by social expectations when selecting activities. They believe they have unlimited options to explore. One girl explained that she consciously chooses to participate in activities to establish her individuality among her friends. Another girl reminded us that "There is a bunch of different groups of girls, and they are accepted. But with the guys, there is one cool group, athletic." "Cool" may also be defined as being completely uninvolved in or aloof from school. One assistant principal told us how the tenth-grade girls hold all of the leadership positions and take part in a variety of school activities, while the boys who are considered "cool" occupy their time by throwing each other into lockers and tossing pinballs down the hallways.

Academic Achievement

Many parents and educators assume that boys outperform girls in school, an assumption due, in part, to the focus of public attention in recent years on how our schools have failed girls. While schools historically have not provided equity and fairness in girls' education, this issue may have obscured another one — that schools have been failing boys as well (Riordan, 1999). Although many Asian and European American boys may achieve at higher rates than girls in such academic areas as mathematics and science and on standardized tests, this is usually the case for only a small minority. While "there is an attention-grabbing handful of star performers, many boys muddle along in the mediocre middle, getting by as average students, and the bottom of the class actually contains a majority of boys rather than girls" (Pollack, 1998). In a recent statewide test in Maryland, girls outperformed boys in every area, with boys of color performing worst of all (Maryland State Department of Education, 1997). The majority of boys strive and achieve academically at average and below average rates, as shown by the following statistics:

- There is a new gender gap, with many boys falling to the bottom of the heap. For reading comprehension, perceptual speed, and word association memory, boys outnumbered girls at the bottom of the scale by a margin of two to one, and many fewer boys than girls scored in the top 10 percent of the groups (U.S. Department of Education, 1997a).

- Although college enrollment for men and women has increased in the last 30 years, the proportion of females enrolling in college has grown at a faster rate than that for males. In 1970, the ratio of male to female college students favored males, by 59 percent to 41 percent; by the 1990s, the ratio had nearly reversed, favoring females by 54 percent to 46 percent (Riordan, 1999).

- Boys in grades 4-8 are twice as likely as girls to be held back a grade, and the rate is even higher for boys of color (U.S. Department of Education, 1996b).

- Boys constitute 71 percent of school suspensions (Pollack, 1998).

- Although the dropout rate is relatively similar for boys and girls, it is significant that Latino and African American students are at greater risk of dropping out than are White students, with Latino students dropping out at a rate more than twice that for White students (U.S. Department of Education, 1996a).

- For African American males, the link typically found between self-esteem and academics may be weakening, in a phenomenon popularly referred to as "dumbing down." A recent study found that, as school achievement decreases, the self-esteem of African American males remains unchanged (Osborne, 1997). This implies that, as students move through school, they become increasingly alienated from academics in order to maintain their self-worth. Our schools and culture discourage African American males from academic or intellectual self-expression.

Learning Disabilities and Special Education

It is alarming that male students are three times as likely as females to be identified as having a learning disability and placed in special education programs (Riordan, 1999). Again, the disparities are even greater for boys of color. Low-income, Latino, and African American male students continue to be placed into low-ability or special education classes at a disproportionate rate — in spite of the extensive research indicating that tracking is not academically sound. A large percentage of our schools serving low-income students and students of color have

51

ineffective educational programs that result in low student performance (The National Coalition of Educational Equity Advocates, 1994; Oakes, 1997; Stone and Roderick, 1995). One reason may be gender and racial stereotyping. The fact that boys are often labeled as hyperactive, aggressive, or in need of special control may explain why so many of them are placed in special education programs even though they may not necessarily have a learning disability (Bushweller, 1994).

It is impossible to draw any hard conclusions about the cause or effect of the learning disability issue on the development of a boy's ability to express his emotions and connect. Although educators have known for a long time that a disproportionate number of males are in special education, few have questioned why, and little research has been conducted in this area. One explanation for the lack of investigation into this problem may be society's view that males are not a minority group and, therefore, don't need intervention. Until we explore and question the biases against boys in our educational system, the special education disparity is likely to continue. New legislation is forcing school systems to address the disproportionate number of African American and Latino males in special education.

Alcohol/Drug Use and Violence

The common belief is that aggressive and destructive behavior is just "boys being boys," that dismissal of a schoolyard fight is acceptable because, with time, boys will outgrow this phase. Youthful acts of violence and alcohol/drug abuse are seen as incidents that happen to others, and aren't our responsibility. After the decade of simplistic solutions, such as "Just Say No!" we entered a period of denial. Now we face the national nightmare of witnessing our children murder each other. The hard truth is that, in recent years, alcohol and drug use and violent crime have escalated for boys and girls, especially among communities of color. In fact, as demonstrated by the following statistics, the violence and drug use in this country increasingly involves young men and boys acting with or against other young men and boys (Pollack, 1998).

- Boys are more likely than girls to report that some of their friends consider it important to engage in delinquent behavior (U.S. Department of Education, 1997b).

- Boys and girls in the eighth grade use drug and alcohol substances at about the same rate. However, boys' frequency of use increases at a faster rate than girls. By the time they're seniors in high school, 7 percent more boys than girls are using marijuana; 8 percent more are using alcohol; and nearly 14 percent more report binge drinking (National Institute on Drug Abuse, 1996).

- High school boys are much more likely to be involved with crime and violence on school property than are girls. Three times as many boys as girls carry weapons to school. Twice as many have been threatened or injured with weapons at school. And twice as many have been in physical fights at school (U.S. Department of Health and Human Services, 1995).

- In general, African American and Latino boys are more likely than other boys to be involved with crime and violence on school property (U.S. Department of Health and Human Services, 1995).

- The death rate for injury by firearms is six times higher for males than for females. Among men, the death rate for injury by firearms is more than twice as high for African American males than for White males (Centers for Disease Control and Prevention, 1997).

- Between 1973 and 1992, the rate of violent victimization of young African American males, ages 12–24, increased about 25 percent. In 1992, the violent victimization rate for African American males, ages 16–19, was almost double the rate for White males and three times that for White females in the same age range. African American males ages 12–24 were almost 14 times as likely to be victims of homicide as members of the general population (U.S. Department of Justice, 1994).

- Within the nation's 75 largest counties in 1994, 92 percent of juveniles who appeared before the criminal courts were male. Two-thirds of the juveniles who appeared in adult criminal court were African American males. African American males comprised the majority of juveniles charged with drug offenses (75 percent) and public-order charges (67 percent). White males comprised the majority of juveniles charged with burglary (82 percent) (U.S. Department of Justice, 1998).

- In 1995, 122 boys were adjudicated as delinquent in the federal courts, 47 percent for either violence- or drug-related offenses. Because the federal government has jurisdiction over certain offenses committed on lands where Native Americans live, 61 percent of juvenile delinquents confined by the Federal Bureau of Prisons were Native Americans (U.S. Department of Justice, 1997).

- There are eight and a half times more males than females in local jails. Over half of these inmates are African American (U.S. Department of Justice, 1997).

This startling statistical evidence suggests an "epidemic" of violent and destructive behavior among many boys. As we have seen in the recent outbreak of shootings in our schools, "Violence is an inspiration to the unstable" (Prothrow-Stith and Weissman, 1991). Risky youthful behaviors, such as drinking, drugs and early outbursts of violence, if unaddressed, often produce men who treat women as objects, and in some situations, who become perpetrators of domestic violence against women (Prothrow-Stith and Weissmann, 1991).

Some social scientists argue that this behavior is the result of "natural aggression" that is coming out in socially unacceptable ways. However, other researchers reject this view, concluding that the current outbreak of teen violence and crime is a new phenomenon (Kantrowitz and Kalb, 1998). Whether this behavior is the result of historical or contemporary

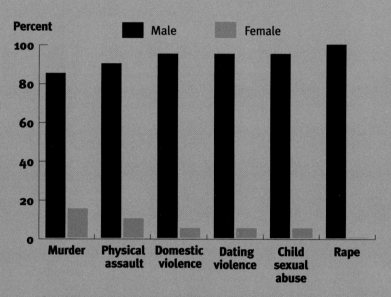

VIOLENCE IS A GENDER ISSUE

Adapted from J. Katz. *Tough Guise: Violence, Media, and the Crisis in Masculinity.*

causes, we must identify early warning signs, search for explanations, work with schools to respond more quickly to these danger signals, and develop strategies for addressing the causes and combating them. Adolescence is a vital time in a child's life. As a parent you must act on your instincts when you see behavior that may become combustible.

Psychological Danger Signals

The veil of masculinity would have us believe that because adolescent and teenage boys don't show it, they don't suffer from depression, that they never feel sad, lonely, or disconnected from others. We know this to be untrue from our focus groups. A majority of the boys with whom we spoke explained that they contend with problems by disconnecting from others and retreating into themselves. One mother explained, "When my son is in real distress he shuts himself away. It's almost like he's protecting me." When asked about coping with sadness, many boys spoke of a need to be alone, isolating themselves from others, and "moving on." Almost universally boys expressed sadness by getting angry. One mother reports, "My son lets a lot of things build up so when they build up sufficiently, his anger explodes." Another father describes his son's reaction to learning of his grandfather's imminent death. "My son almost never articulated his feelings about Dad's illness. But when we told him his grandfather was getting worse, he attacked us for saying it was true."

> One mother reported that the father of one of Justin's very good friends died suddenly and unexpectedly. After trying to call him by telephone, he was finally able to reach him. Justin was comforted when his grieving friend assured him, "He wasn't going to let it depress him."

In our focus groups, boys explained that their method of coping with emotional problems existed within the boundaries of preserving their independence. They worry that if they share a problem or emotions with a parent or other adult, they will be bombarded with questions and advice. Boys fear they will be forever defined by the problem, so their instinct is not to open up. One father, recalling his own adolescence, stated, "My own parents used to wonder what I did in my room. They still talk about it. I was always nice to them but I would not tell them a damn thing about my life. I never communicated deep feelings to them for eight years." Another father, speaking of his son, commented, "He shuts down about school. Sometimes any question is too many questions." A mother commented, "I don't know what makes my son sad. I can tell when he

It was hard for a lot of these old men to ask for help or to accept it when it was offered. They had been so strong so long, and all of a sudden they couldn't hardly get to the grocery store. It scared them first and then it made them angry, a typical black male pattern, if you think about it. Brothers tend to be more familiar with anger than any of their other emotions, so if you leave them to their own devices, that's usually where they'll go. It can start out as fear, or confusion, or sorrow, or hurt feelings, but nine times out of ten, it's going to come out on the other end mad. Sometimes you can talk them out of it if you catch it on the front end, but the process requires lightning reflexes, infinite patience, and nerves of steel.

—*Pearl Cleage, What Looks Like Crazy on an Ordinary Day*

is angry or happy. I can't tell when he is sad." This emotional isolation makes it difficult for adults to become aware of boys' suffering or accurately distinguish between depression and a desire for privacy.

> People who are frailer, less stable, are more subject to the dark images they see. Teenagers, who are, by nature in greater thrall to sweeps of emotion and sadness, are most vulnerable. —*Peggy Noonan, "The Culture of Death"*

It is important for parents to recognize and respect the ways boys cope with problems. The techniques employed successfully with our daughters may not work with our sons. For example, girls tend to experience their emotions more directly and openly. One mother reported to us how fortunate she was to have her son in a coed carpool. She said she found out things about her son and his friends while driving the carpool because the girls talked openly about almost everything. Parents cannot necessarily expect such openness from their sons. As one teacher described it, "Girls are taught early on to talk through their problems, while boys are still taught to be tough."

We must learn to pick up the unique cues our sons give us about their feelings of sadness and react appropriately to the situation. One strategy that seems to work for the parents with whom we spoke is to model appropriate empathetic behavior by discussing their feelings with their sons. One mother told us, "I let him know when he has hurt my feelings, and if he knows that I'm justified, then he feels terrible, but I try to get him to communicate this emotional response to me. Sometimes I only know intuitively that he feels bad. He won't talk to me, he won't deal with his sadness or hurt feelings until he can be unemotional about it, and say, 'I'm really sorry;' but he has to go past that point of hurt." Boys have to be taught about emotions and the importance of communicating their feelings.

The statistics on suicide provide us with confirming evidence of the extent to which boys suffer undiagnosed depression. Until boys and girls are nine years old, their suicide rates are identical. But from the ages of 10–14, the suicide rate for boys is twice the rate for girls (U.S. Department of Health and Human Services, 1995). Between the ages

A depressed, insecure child is one thing, and quite common. But that same boy with a gun can be a lethal threat. In all of the recent shootings, acquiring guns was easier than buying beer, or even gas. —*Timothy Egan*, *"From Adolescent Angst to Shooting Up Schools"*

of 15 and 24, the rate is six times as high. Although figures have increased most dramatically for African American males ages 10–14, White males commit suicide at a slightly higher rate than African American males (Anderson, Kochanek, and Murphy, 1995).

Furthermore, although females are twice as likely to try suicide as males, the completion rate is higher for males in all groups, ranging from two to six times that attempted by females. Some theorize that this is due to the method of choice. Firearms are used in 60 percent of male suicide cases, while pills are employed most frequently by females (National Institute of Mental Health, 1996). Again, we are confronted with the effects of unaddressed alienation and resulting violence. Male suicide attempts are more aggressive, and thus more likely to be final. Females rely on less aggressive methods, so they can frequently be saved. It's as though females use suicide as the classic "cry for help," while males use it as a perceived last resort, when they feel there is no hope and no way out.

STARTLING STATEMENTS

We hope you now know what it is really like to be an adolescent boy today. To check your understanding, we've compiled a list of "startling statements." See how many of them you can estimate correctly.

1. Teenage boys do an average of _____ hours of homework at home each week, while their teenage sisters do an average of _____ hours of work.

2. Boys are more likely to be diagnosed as learning disabled, ADHD and autistic than girls. T F

3. Dropout rates for African American male students have increased since 1990. What percent have they reached? _____ percent

4. Because of the widespread attitude that Asians are academically successful, many schools don't monitor or even record the dropout rates among Asian-Pacific students. T F

5. Boys constitute _____ percent of school suspensions.

6. Adolescent boys show a significantly higher rate of drug and alcohol abuse than girls. T F

7. By 2020, it is projected that more than 1 in _____ children in the United States will be of Hispanic origin.

8. In 1998, _____ percent of White, non-Hispanic children lived with two parents, compared with _____ percent of Black children and _____ percent of children of Hispanic origin.

9. Most children in poverty are White, non-Hispanics. However, the proportion of Black or Hispanic children in poverty is much higher than the proportion for White, non-Hispanic children. T F

10. Boys have consistently higher reading scores than girls at all ages. T F

11. What percent of Japanese students are in the bottom quartile on standardized tests? _____ percent

12. Firearms were the most frequent weapon used in suicides and homicides among adolescent males. T F

13. Men live, on the average, almost _____ years less than women.

References:

Children's Defense Fund, 1997.

Federal Interagency Forum on Child and Family Statistics, 1999.

Kim,H, 1997.

National Urban League, 1998.

Prince Georges County Public Schools, 1999.

Walker-Moffat, W., 1995.

Answers:

1.	3, 10	8.	76%, 36%, 64%
2.	True	9.	True
3.	17.5%	10.	False
4.	True	11.	30%
5.	71%	12.	True
6.	True	13.	10
7.	5		

Focus on Adolescent Males of Color
What Cultural Factors Affect the Development of African American, Asian, and Latino Teenage Boys to Form and Sustain Connections with Parents, Schools, and Friends?

Overview

To understand boys more fully, we need to explore what roles race and culture play in their daily lives. This is an important exploration for all parents because we have multiple identities and need to understand their value. African American, Asian, and Latino male adolescents have much in common with their European American male counterparts in their attitudes concerning relationships with family, school, and their peers. While information about Native American boys is included in the research findings, they were not present in our focus groups, and they are absent from much of the current literature. Some similarities of all the boys we interviewed include:

- valuing family relationships
- importance of peer group support
- attachments to symbols of teenage boys
  (e.g., clothes, music, specific interests)
- judgments of other teens on the basis of these symbols
- importance of having girls as friends and confidants
- using anger as a response to sadness and loneliness
- relying on short conversations
- needing privacy
- discomfort with probing questions
- defining masculinity as a reaction to femininity

In a recent study, Whites and African Americans were asked, "How often does race come into your mind as something that is going to affect what happens to you today?" Among Whites, 2 percent said "often" and among African Americans it was at least 65 percent who said, "virtually every day." So the added element of dealing with racism always has to be factored into the equation.

—*James Gilligan, Violence: Reflections on a National Epidemic*

While there are similarities among all male adolescents, we know that differences in race/ethnicity, culture, and socioeconomic status do play a significant role in shaping how they relate to peers, family, school, and the development of identity. To detail the complex interplay of each diverse culture on the formation of connections to each of these important aspects of boys' lives is far beyond the scope of this book. At the same time, we would be remiss in not discussing some of the factors linked to issues of race/ethnicity, culture, and socioeconomic status that influence an adolescent boy's social, emotional, and academic development.

In this chapter, we discuss how mainstream culture and the home and community cultures of ethnically and racially diverse adolescents help to shape their identities and their relationships with peers, school, their parents, and the larger society. Our goal is to illustrate some of the challenges and conflicts boys encounter in developing their identity and relationships, and to discuss some of the strategies and support systems within each culture that they use to navigate mainstream culture. It is clear that, for the boys in our focus groups, the strength and resiliency gained from the traditions of their ethnic and cultural heritage help to mitigate many of the problems they face.

Remaining anchored in a positive sense of one's cultural identity in the face of racism is an antidote to alienation and despair. —Beverly Daniel Tatum, Why Are All the Black Kids Sitting Together in the Cafeteria?

Developing Identity

Although mainstream culture tends to homogenize teenagers, all individuals have multifaceted identities that shape who we ultimately become. In the mix of these identities is racial group identity, which for adolescents from diverse ethnic and cultural backgrounds, is an extremely important part of the development of their sense of self. As such, adolescents from diverse ethnic and cultural backgrounds are more likely than White adolescents to actively engage in exploring their racial/ethnic and cultural identity (Tatum, 1997). African American teenagers, in particular, often see themselves in relation to their race/ethnicity or cultural identity because, in part, that's how a large part of their world views them. A similar process is found among Latino, Native American, and Asian adolescent boys (Tatum, 1997).

The identity development of all children, boys and girls, White and from diverse racial/ethnic and cultural backgrounds, depends on many factors and is influenced by individuals, families, communities, culture, institutions, history, and racial dynamics. Parents and educators need to value and understand the special conditions that create the variety of experiences that shape our children's identities.

Oppositional Identity, Academic Achievement, and Peer Pressure

Adolescent males from diverse ethnic and cultural groups are often forced to choose between their racial/ethnic and cultural group identity and attainment of "success," especially when "success" is defined by academic achievement and peer group membership. In response to this dilemma, many adolescents take on the false mantle of an oppositional identity. Oppositional identity occurs when a child does the opposite of what is expected of him. As Comer and Poussaint (1992) describe it, "Stop running!" causes more running and "Hurry up!" brings a slowdown. The oppositional identity can become a problem and it can seriously affect academic achievement and relationships between parents and children and children and their peers. It can also affect children's interactions with the larger society, including the media and the juvenile and criminal justice systems. Culturally dissonant pressures, expectations, and conflicts among home, community, school, and mainstream culture may promote misinformed, unhealthy, and unfair choices for adolescents from diverse ethnic and cultural backgrounds.

Even though making and maintaining friends from one's own racial/ethnic group is an important and healthy part of adolescent development, the process of choosing between friends and academic achievement can and often does become oppositional. In part because of inadequate access to positive role models — especially in the classroom — and exposure to the rich history of African American intellectualism, many African American children believe that to preserve and promote the value of their own identity, they must reject academic achievement (Tatum, 1997). African Americans' devaluing of education and academic achievement appears to be entirely a post-desegregation phenomenon (Tatum, 1997). Prior to school desegregation, achievement was considered to be a common experience in all Black schools.

While not all youth of African descent feel this way about achieving in school, this response is not totally unexpected, given the many African American children who are tracked into lower-level academic programs, and thus, who have difficulty achieving success in school. In the experience of many African American children, the culture of American schools has identified achievers as being White (Oakes, et al., 1997; Ford, 1996; National Research Council, 1997; U.S. Department of Education, 1994).

...the anger and resentment that adolescents feel in response to their growing awareness of the systematic exclusion of Black people from full participation in U.S. society leads to the development of an oppositional social identity. This oppositional stance protects one's identity from the psychological assault of racism and keeps that dominant group at a distance. —*Beverly Daniel Tatum, Why Are All the Black Kids Sitting Together in the Cafeteria?*

Many ethnically and culturally diverse teenage boys feel pressured to choose between involvement in their own culture and cultural groups and the expectations of mainstream culture. For example, in one of our focus groups, an African American teenager told us that to feel good about achieving in high school, he doesn't hang out with other African American kids because they view achieving in school as "acting White."

Another African American adolescent told us that as he got older and continued to hang out with his White friends from childhood, he was often ignored by his African American peers. As he became more involved in school activities that were dominated by White students, he struggled with integrating his two groups of friends. He felt that his African American friends viewed his identification with White students as a rejection of them and his African American identity.

Grappling with a similar issue, a Latino mother in one of our focus groups shared: "Spanish kids have a stigma. It is often assumed that Latino kids are underachievers. I have struggled with my son in dealing with this stereotype about low academic achievement. He tries to ignore it, and I tell him it's okay to be different. It's okay to be Latino, it's okay to be an 'A' student, not only okay, but I expect him to be an 'A' student." Her son does not want to be associated with being Latino because Latino students are often defined as being academically inferior. His mother struggles to support both his academic achievement and his comfort with his Latino heritage.

Success in our society is often defined by acceptance of White norms and expectations. At the same time, males of color are often blocked from achieving "success" according to these standards by institutional racism and prejudice. However, not all adolescents from culturally and linguistically diverse backgrounds seem to follow the same pattern. In their work in underachievement of students from diverse ethnic and cultural groups, Fordham and Ogbu (1986) make the distinction between voluntary and involuntary cultures. They hypothesize that the assimilation process is considerably less painful for groups that have chosen to come to the United States. Many of these immigrants are escaping war, oppression, and/or poverty in their homelands, but arrive in this country with a strong sense of ethnic identity and culture intact.

African American adolescents often fall into the involuntary group, particularly those whose heritage descends in part from slaves who were brought to this country under the harshest of conditions. Native American students also fall into this group, because they have to grow up with a heritage that includes dispossession and culture clash. Having been severed from their cultures and languages during centuries of slavery and oppression, African Americans and Native Americans as a whole are engaged in a continual process of preserving, recapturing, rediscovering, and redefining their identities and culture.

In addition to inheriting a legacy of multigenerational disenfranchisement and discrimination, adolescence naturally awakens an awareness of the presence of institutional racism. Therefore, it shouldn't be surprising that African American and Native American adolescents are more likely to have negative feelings about mainstream culture (Tatum, 1997). Furthermore, under some circumstances, boys from low-income families embrace both their heritage and the negative academic definitions of themselves. In response, they may turn to gangs for support against prejudice and their perception of the outside world as "culturally alien, threatening, and impenetrable" (Belitz and Valdez, 1995; Jackson, 1998).

Coming of Age

One way some Latino and African American adolescents demonstrate "toughness," often associated with "being a man," is to adopt a super-masculine identity. In some communities, toughness can be an important survival skill. For Latinos, this concept is known as machismo, which also has its roots in Latin American culture (Casas, et al., 1995). One Latino mother said, "They [her sons] want to show off to their friends how tough they can be, they don't want to accept that they are adolescent boys." However, "toughness" and "machismo" are often in conflict with the norms of accepted school behavior.

Various ethnic and cultural groups around the world often conduct "rites of passage" that affirm the value of young people in the society and introduce them to the responsibilities and obligations of adulthood. In the past, culturally based rituals and traditions have provided young people with a connection to their culture. Caring adults and a like community of peers have helped them in their search for purpose and meaning, and in their educational and career success. Attempting to capture the promise of their adolescent youth, many ethnically diverse communities and organizations are establishing programs for adolescent males that focus on social, academic, and economic development.

These programs include "rite of passage" ceremonies that affirm the journey toward manhood in positive and healthy ways. In addition, extended families provide models of cultural traditions that serve to create a safe haven and expose males of color to positive role models.

These relationships create intimate connections as boys move through adolescence. In Latino communities, young adults work with adolescents and act as "culture brokers," teaching them to be bicultural, and "passing on their understanding of community traditions, while helping them to succeed in schools, colleges, and communities at large" (Cooper, Denner, and Lopez, 1999).

Fathers and Sons

Children are raised in different kinds of families, too many without fathers, others with traditional fathers, and still others with fathers who are taking on more active roles in the family. Children live in homes with biological fathers, stepfathers, adoptive fathers, part-time fathers, or no fathers. But what's clear is that fathers play important emotional and intellectual roles in the development of both male and female children. Fathers also make important contributions to how and what boys learn about becoming men.

In 1998, however, more than 51 percent of African American and 27 percent of Latino American children under the age of 18 lived in mother-only households (compared with 18 percent of White children) (Federal Interagency Forum on Child and Family Statistics, 1999). Given the importance of a father's presence and involvement to all children, it is logical to conclude that the absence of fathers in the African and Latino communities — for a variety of reasons — has had a wide-ranging and profound effect on the social and emotional development of many adolescent males in these communities.

> **What I see is a tremendous readiness in men to actually speak about their experience, have some empathy for what happened to them as boys, and resolve to do better for boys.... —Michael Thompson, "Boys to Men: Questions of Violence"**

Just as fathers who are absent from children's lives can create challenges for those children in growing up, changes in the roles of fathers who choose to participate more actively in family life can also benefit and add challenges to the father-son relationships. Some fathers who haven't experienced much emotional communication with their own fathers are anxious to learn how to communicate better with their sons. One mother expressed this sentiment when she asked, "How can we help teach our kids communication skills so that when they are fathers, they can communicate with their boys?"

Ethnically and Culturally Diverse Adolescents and Society

One African American mother told us that her son tries to include his best friend — who is African American — in his mostly White peer group, but this friend refuses to join them, so her son only sees this friend alone. Racial stereotyping fosters tensions not only within groups of ethnically and culturally diverse males, but between different groups of ethnically and culturally diverse males as well. One mother explains, "There are multiple dimensions to discrimination, it doesn't have to be Black versus White, it can also be Black versus Latino, Black versus Black, Latino versus Asian."

For example, the "model minority" stereotype of Asians in the United States has served to pit them against other people of color who are also affected by racism. Asians, to some extent, are perceived as "White" due to their perceived privileged status in society. However, a close look at the statistics indicates that many Asian groups are not as privileged as is believed, and they are also victimized by racism.

One Asian mother explains that her son talks about how embarrassed he feels because he isn't good in math or science. She says, "My son tells me that his teachers expect him to perform at a higher level than he feels he can, and this makes him feel bad." Because of this misperception, Asian adolescents are often the targets of stereotyping by adults and racially based taunting and harassment by other students (Tatum, 1997).

Black and Hispanic boys can experience particular problems in adolescence, researchers say, because when they act peer-pleasingly tough, adults see them as dangerous and threatening, but if they act soft, they are likelier to be victimized.

— *Carey Goldberg, "Growing Move to Address a Cultural Threat to Boys"*

We can't underestimate the difficulties that young males from diverse ethnic and cultural groups have in trying to achieve the "right" balance in their relationships with parents, peers, schooling, and other important aspects of their communities. Parents confirm over and over that while they do value education, the challenges of raising their sons in an often misunderstanding and judgmental world comes into conflict with being successful in school. One mother said, "My son needs to be tough, but tough doesn't make it in school."

It isn't just "tough boys" who are at risk. Another mother shares: "I always worry about my son being in the wrong place at the wrong time. He's a good boy, but other people don't see that. They see that he's Black." This perception was confirmed by many African American teenagers in the focus groups.

For example, one of the boys reported, "Because I am big, 6 feet, 200 pounds, and very dark-skinned, people find me threatening and walk away from me. In the mall, the guys who work there always look at me and my friends with suspicion, as if we're there to make trouble." The environment for boys changes in adolescence, and people who previously found them to be unthreatening now begin to move out of their way. For many boys, the cycle of racism becomes apparent. Parents reported over and over again a fear of their sons being targets of racism. One African American mother reported, "I teach my son survival skills as a protection against racism." This fear presents parents with the overwhelming responsibility of trying to prepare their sons to be independent, while, at the same time, wanting desperately to protect them from possible harassment or harm.

Institutional Racism in Schools

Our children spend many of their formative years in the public education system, often facing institutional racial bias in their individual schools and the system at large. The evidence of this racial bias is multidimensional and is present in almost all schools with an ethnically and culturally diverse student body. Racial bias is particularly easy to see in integrated public schools. Walk into any such high school and check the participation of kids in extracurricular activities where the students choose their own groups. Parents in the focus groups expressed concern about the amount of self-segregation they see their children doing, even though they attend integrated schools. Although this self-segregation is a normal and natural progression in children's development of their own racial identity, it can also be symptomatic of institutional racial bias within the school setting (Tatum, 1997). How can we know if segregation is the result of the choice to affirm positive racial identity or the result of institutional racism that can lead to negative identities, oppositional attitudes, and/or gang affiliation?

Racial bias is regularly institutionalized in class assignments and within the school culture, both of which promote this self-segregation. As a result, ethnically and culturally diverse boys tend to underachieve, are disproportionately represented in special education classes, have low participation in non-athletic extracurricular activities, and are under-represented in advanced classes (National Urban League, 1998). One teenage boy in our focus groups said, "Even though my school has many students of color, I am often the only Black in honors classes. I find that strange."

Another African American adolescent told this story: "Because I'm tall, the first question adults ask me is if I am on the varsity basketball team. They're trying to make conversation with me. I'm tired of answering that question." With narrow choices and racial stereotyping, it's no wonder that many boys of color don't do well in traditional public schools.

As a result of institutionalized racial bias, adolescents from ethnically and culturally diverse groups fare poorly in school, compared with their White peers. They typically score lower on both the verbal and mathematics portions of the SAT; attain proficiency in reading, math, and science at significantly lower levels; and consistently score lower on the national test of writing abilities, regardless of grade level (The College Board, 1999; Donahue et al., 1999; National Center for Education Statistics, 1998). Males from diverse ethnic and cultural groups also have higher dropout rates than White males (U.S. Department of Education, 1996a).

When viewed as a large, homogeneous group, Asians seem to perform well in school. However, this is decidedly untrue for certain Asian ethnic groups, most notably Southeast Asians, which include Vietnamese, Cambodians, Laotians, and Hmongs. For these ethnic groups, the "model minority" stereotype has a negative effect because administrators and teachers tend to ignore their very real schooling needs and requirements, with serious consequences. Dropout rates among these Asian ethnic groups highlight our failure to address their learning needs adequately. Dropout rates for schools with large concentrations of Southeast Asians are approximately 50 percent. In 1992, the dropout rate for Filipinos was 46 percent. For Samoans, it was 60 percent. Like their African American and Latino peers, high numbers of Southeast Asians (35 percent) and Japanese (30 percent) also fail to do well in reading, with scores in the bottom quartile on standardized reading tests (Kim, 1997).

Problems with academic achievement often lead to difficulties in relationships between parents and their children and children and their peers (Casas, et al., 1995; Comer and Poussaint, 1992). Conflicts that come about as a result of children not doing well in school may lead them to become estranged from their parents and society and can plant the seeds of unhealthy social and emotional behavior.

Although academic achievement is highly correlated with the income and educational levels of children's parents, racial bias in the educational environment is also considered by many to be an important factor in underachievement of ethnically and culturally diverse students. Evidence of the potential of racial bias as a factor in academic achievement can be seen in some of the startling new data about underachievement of middle-class African American males.

SAT scores for 1995 showed that Black students whose parents had at least one graduate degree averaged 191 points lower than White students whose parents had the same amount of education. This gap is even larger than the one between Black and White students whose parents had no high school diploma — 137 points on average (Belluck, 1999).

1995 SAT SCORES SEPARATED BY RACE AND EDUCATION LEVEL OF PARENTS

Race	No parent with high school degree	At least one parent with graduate degree
Black	655	844
White	792	1035
Difference	-137	-191

Developed by The Mid-Atlantic Equity Center, Chevy Chase, MD, 1999.

This disparity in achievement between Black and White students with similar parental income and education levels can be seen in achievement statistics from Shaker Heights High School, an academically acclaimed school just outside Cleveland, Ohio. Although most Black and White families in Shaker Heights are solidly middle class, African American students, who make up half the student population, constituted only 9 percent of those who graduated in the top fifth of their class, but 83 percent of those in the bottom fifth (Belluck, 1999).

Chronic underachievement among minority students is one of the most critical problems facing our country today. It is particularly troubling because we are not just talking about disadvantaged youngsters. Even minority students from relatively wealthy families with well-educated parents do not typically perform as well as White and Asian students from similar backgrounds. —Gaston Caperton, The College Board President. ©1999 by The College Entrance Examination Board

There are many hypotheses to explain this middle-class gap. They include lower teacher expectations, peer pressure against "acting White," the newness of middle-class status among Black families, and a lack of parental involvement with parents who assume that, once they send their child to a "good" school, the school will take care of the child. Increasingly, the hypotheses also include institutional racial bias.

Whatever the cause of widespread poor academic performance among ethnically and culturally diverse students, "The bottom line is that if African Americans, Hispanics, and Native Americans are to reach overall educational parity with Whites or Asians, including among top students, ways must be found to improve academic outcomes for all of their social class segments" (The College Board, 1999). It's clear that males of color, whatever their socioeconomic status, experience significant additional stresses as they move through adolescence into manhood. However, ethnically and culturally diverse individuals also have the resources of their rich heritage and family relationships to help mentor and support them along the way.

Culture Clash — Children, Families, School, Communities, and the Media

The mainstream culture exemplified in schools and in the media often differs from the home and community cultures of males from diverse ethnic and cultural backgrounds. This disparity may cause these adolescent boys to feel alienated from both cultures. One Latino youth spoke to this issue in relation to speaking Spanish. He acknowledged that mainstream culture did not value speaking a different language and, to fit in, he "began to speak Spanish less and less at home." He said that since both of his parents spoke only Spanish, "gradually me and my parents stopped speaking to each other." As boys become more immersed in an English-only culture, they gradually stop speaking to their parents (Tatum, 1997). It's difficult to stay connected with one's parents if you don't speak the same language.

While some of the children avoid speaking their native language, many parents hoped that their children would appreciate the "magnificence of their language and the advantages of being bilingual." In fact, some of the boys we spoke with are struggling to reclaim their language. Given the important connection between language and the development of identity, families and schools must encourage and support children in their efforts to become bilingual and bicultural.

This scenario is further complicated in circumstances where the parents do not speak English, and the child functions as an interpreter for the family. In this case, the child is aware that he plays a vital role, but may not feel that his role is sufficiently valued or respected when he is not offered any influence on the actual decision-making within his family.

In many cases, values and principles that are affirmed in mainstream society and the classroom are at odds with those practiced in the home. For instance, East Asian cultures embody a strong sense of *filial piety* — children not only must obey their parents but also must not challenge their judgment or authority. In East Asian societies, this strong sense of filial piety is integrated into the teachings and practices of the schools, so there is no structural conflict between the school and home environments. However, in American schools, children are generally taught to believe that inquiry and debate are good practices, and that right versus wrong is determined by reason.

Another example of these differences in values is demonstrated by the concept of privacy in Latino culture. One Latino mother explained that in her culture, "Privacy is almost nonexistent. All the parents knew what you were going to do. All your friends knew every single detail. And you weren't allowed to keep secrets. I was shocked when I saw the sense of independence and privacy that teenagers have in this country. The teenagers expect and demand independence and privacy from their parents. This is my place, this is my room, this is my program on television, this is my time with my friends. In our country, it was 'ours' and 'us,' the concept of mine is very different."

Thus, teenagers may disagree with their parents and want to challenge them, but are considered disrespectful when they do so. This may make the child feel alienated and reduce communication between the child and parent. However, if children can learn to feel comfortable in both cultures, this integration may increase communication between parents and children and among their peers.

How the news media and entertainment industry affect the thinking and beliefs of adolescent boys is not easily quantifiable, but their influence in society is so pervasive that many parents believe, as one African American mother said, "Sex and violence are so present in our son's everyday life that they are really distorting the way he is growing up."

In addition, the news media and entertainment industry perpetuate negative stereotypes and false beliefs about ethnically and culturally diverse males, and continue to under-portray certain racial/ethnic groups as positive role models. Media watch groups such as Fairness and Accuracy in Reporting (FAIR), the Center for Media and Public Affairs (CMPA), the NewsWatch Project, MediaWatch, and the Media Action Network for Asian Americans (MANAA) have pointed out many examples of this discrimination.

For example, the physical size of male action film stars, the physique of male action figures, and the images of rock and rap performers establish the "real man" as a "rugged individualist, which means you don't complain, you don't admit weakness, you don't ever let others see the anxious man behind the curtain." The concept of the "cool pose," which allows young males to "strike a pose of cool, badness, or violence," appeals to boys living in the suburbs and in the cities (Majors and Billson, 1992; Katz and Jhally, 1999).

> **Across race and gender, the majority of children believe that the boys and men they see on television are different from themselves, boys that they know, their fathers, and other adult male relatives.** — *Children Now, "Boys to Men: Messages About Masculinity"*

The proportion of African American and Latino characters in television and film is still far below their numbers in the real world. When they are present, they tend to be isolated characters or are highly stereotyped. Few television series portray African American, Latino, Native American, or Asian characters as powerful, prosperous, well-educated, and authoritative (Lichter, et al., 1994).

The media also claim that Asian people in the United States are "foreign" and not "American." This assumption is made, even though many second-, third-, and fourth-generation Asian immigrants are highly assimilated into mainstream culture and speak English with no trace of a foreign accent. This bias is reflected in and propagated by media and entertainment industries that show a disproportionate number of Asian characters speaking with foreign accents and broken English. In many cases, Asian American personalities are portrayed by comedians and actors as speaking with accents, even though their actual speech patterns and accents are distinctively "American" (Media Action Network for Asian Americans, 1999).

We can easily infer how media biases, like the ones described above, may damage the cognitive and emotional development of boys from ethnically and culturally diverse groups. This damage occurs because the media paint a picture of the world in which people of color are not equal participants, and where they are seen as less worthy and valuable to society than are Whites. Cultural theorist Raymond Williams goes even further, arguing that the image on television, billboards, in video games and film "produces us. We don't simply make our way through the thousands of images we see daily and pick and choose what we like and don't like. These images have a profound impact on our tastes, attitudes, and the kinds of choices we make" (Katz and Jhally, 1999).

Sports play a significant role in breaking down some of these stereotypes, because they seem to be the great equalizer among White boys and boys from diverse cultural and ethnic backgrounds. It's clear from the focus groups that boys engage in cross-cultural friendships in and outside of school through team sports. We should take advantage of this opportunity to foster cross-cultural dialogues. We must also provide non-athletic opportunities for males from diverse ethnic and cultural backgrounds to excel and to hold leadership positions. Schools must take a more proactive role in correcting the belief that to achieve academically or to participate in other school-related extracurricular activities is to "act White."

When boys are not validated, they disconnect and turn to someone who understands them. If there's no caring and involved adult in their lives, these boys turn to their peers and inappropriate adult role models. The peer group defines for them what is appropriately "Black," "Asian," "Latino," or "Native American." Unfortunately, for many ethnically and culturally diverse males, this means that "to behave in the manner defined as falling within a White cultural frame of reference is to 'act White' and is negatively sanctioned" (Fordham and Ogbu, 1986). Along with their peer group, the media define for these boys what it means to be a culturally and ethnically diverse male in this society. The way the media, both print and non-print, portray ethnically and culturally diverse males only exacerbates their alienation and further confuses their understanding of how they fit into society.

It is not surprising that, with these outside negative influences, parents are asking, "How can I help my child?" "How can I struggle with these issues in addition to helping my child grow up?" The parents with whom we spoke were philosophical in their search for answers. One African American mother reminded us all: "There are lessons to learn and lessons to teach." An important lesson to teach is that everyone involved in the growth, development, and learning of teenagers must support their efforts to become emissaries and role models, so that they are defined by more than their separateness. If children are exposed at an early age to images of successful individuals from diverse cultural and ethnic backgrounds, then they don't have to define success in school as being "for Whites only."

While we value diversity in friendships, we must acknowledge that the process of developing and affirming one's ethnic and cultural identity is essential to a positive sense of self. A model of adolescent development, as defined by Jean Phinney, can be applied to all people of diverse ethnic and cultural backgrounds who share similar patterns of racial, ethnic, or cultural oppression (Tatum, 1997). The three stages are: 1) unexamined ethnic identity, when race or ethnicity is not particularly important (pre-teen boys); 2) ethnic identity search, when members are actively involved in understanding what it means to be part of a group (teenage boys fall into this stage); and 3) achieved ethnic identity, when an ethnic or cultural identity is internalized (Tatum, 1997).

Tatum uses this model to explain that, when we see racial groups separate themselves in the cafeteria, it's not always the result of the perceived racism of the school. It can be a confirmation of ethnic identity. We need to understand that this is an important part of adolescent development, while at the same time, we create opportunities for adolescent males to choose among a wider range of options.

Ethnic identity is a complex issue, and we don't pretend to know or discuss all of its complexities. However, it's important to acknowledge this factor as another piece of the puzzle of understanding the challenges faced by males from diverse ethnic and cultural backgrounds in this society and their impact on making connections.

SHAPING YOUR OWN IDENTITY

The following questionnaire is designed to help you identify messages that you received as you were growing up as a member of your own racial/ethnic group. Please answer each of the following with as many messages as you can remember.

Describe your racial/ethnic/cultural group: Asian American, African American, Hispanic/Latin American, American Indian, European American, or _____ .

1. Things I was encouraged to believe about my people.

2. Things I was discouraged from believing about people of my racial/ethnic/cultural group.

3. Ways I was taught (instructed, shown, experienced) that my people dealt with strong feelings or emotions, such as affection and anger.

4. Ways I was taught that my people thought/behaved regarding school and work/career.

5. Values stressed to me about how good a person of my racial/ethnic/cultural group should behave/appear.

6. Ways I was taught to interact with people who were of other racial/ethnic/cultural groups.

7. Things I was taught (instructed, shown, experienced) about people of other racial/ethnic/cultural groups (identify the group).

8. Ways I was taught people of other racial/ethnic/cultural groups behaved regarding school and work/career.

9. People of my racial/ethnic/cultural group that I was encouraged to view as role models and why.

10. People of other racial/ethnic/cultural groups I was encouraged to view as role models and why.

11. Ways in which I was expected to make positive contributions to my racial/ethnic/cultural group.

Which of the above messages have had the most lasting effect on you and why?

Which of the above messages have had the most negative effect on you? Positive effect? Why?

Adapted with permission from Hardiman, Jackson and Kim. Growing Up Racially.©1986

> **In times of rapid cultural change... strong ties with family elders sustain access to wisdom and cultural traditions.** —*Catherine Cooper, Jill Denner, and Edward Lopez, "Cultural Brokers: Helping Latino Children on Pathways Toward Success"*

Understanding where we come from and what messages have influenced us through our growing-up years and now as adults helps to prepare and sustain us in our roles as parents. In reflecting on your answers, we hope you will see the positive side of ethnic and cultural diversity and be able to recognize the issues of culture that may be present in your life and in the lives of others who collide with the diverse and mainstream societies. Our sons are struggling to live in the context of the rules and expectations of many diverse cultures, and these circumstances create benefits and challenges as we guide them through adolescence to young adulthood.

A Work in Progress
Why Is It Difficult to Create More Than Just a "Few Good Men"?

I n *The Courage to Raise Good Men,* Olga Silverstein and Beth Rashbaum (1994) observe that in the current culture, each sex is asked to "halve itself." In other words, each gender is expected to express only specific emotions. These expectations are influenced not only by gender, but by culture and socioeconomic class as well. For example, some girls are expected to inhibit assertiveness while some boys are expected to inhibit their capacity for intimacy. African American girls are socialized to be strong, independent, and assertive, as well as nurturing and valuing family (Hall, 1999). African American boys might express their masculinity by discarding what is traditionally valued by a Eurocentric society, and may "reject the importance of conventional norms like getting a good education and focusing on…a 'cool pose' as alternative sources of esteem" (Majors and Billson, 1992; Fordham and Ogbu, 1986). But what many of these boys have in common is a culture that supports the cutting off of emotions in men at an early age (Silverstein and Rashbaum, 1994). Consider the phrase, "A daughter is a daughter for life, a boy is a son until he takes a wife." Think about what this phrase communicates. It normalizes the expected abrupt break of the emotional bond between a boy and his family, and communicates to parents that they need to prepare their son for his leaving.

> We have to build a culture that doesn't reward that separation from the person who raised them. — *Michael Norman, "From Carol Gilligan's Chair."*

One mother, with a 16-year-old son and a son who is a college freshman, told the story of her older son asking both parents to come to school to help him move from his dorm to his first apartment. She was surprised by his request because he's so organized and independent. She even

asked whether he only wanted his dad, because he's so good with tools. Her son had to repeat, "No, I just want you to be there." The mother said she finally got it; he didn't want to move into his apartment alone. She reflected on how differently she would have responded if this were a college-age daughter. The fathers in the focus group seemed to support this observation. As one father described, "I like it when my son has strong views and is independent. I would rather see him appear in control than to worry that he doesn't feel in control." Moderation doesn't seem to be an option for boys in our culture.

Mothers often are made to feel uncomfortable when they get too close to their sons, and boys can feel their mothers pulling away. One mother reported that when her older son was having problems and seeing a therapist, "One of the first things the therapist said to me was that I have to step back." There is a fear that if a son is close to his mother, he won't become a "real man." Because we live in a society that warns mothers about being too close to their sons, it's difficult to ignore these messages. On the one hand, we ask 1990s boys to be caring and sensitive and then, at the same time, saddle them with society's rigid cultural norms and stereotypes about masculinity.

These norms dictate that boys must learn to be stoic, tough, competitive, goal-oriented, driven, and invincible. One mother articulated her confusion about this issue through her feelings concerning her son. She explained that she is both pleased and concerned that her son has an easygoing temperament. When she thought about her reaction to his behavior, this mother admitted she has a double standard. She worried that her one-year-old son won't be tough enough to protect himself in the world. However, she understood that if her child was a girl, she would value, indeed prefer, the baby's easygoing behavior and temperament. Because he's a boy, she worried that he would need to be

In a culture of ornament, manhood is defined by appearance, by youth and attractiveness, by money and aggression, by posture and swagger and "props," by the curled lip and flexed biceps, by the glamour of the cover boy and by the market-bartered "individuality" that sets one astronaut or athlete or gangster above another.
—*Susan Faludi, "The Betrayal of the American Man"*

aggressive and tough. Such expectations are present throughout society. It wasn't so long ago that, "It looked like American politician Edmund Muskie had a lock on the Democratic nomination for the 1972 presidential race, until he started to cry in responding to newspaper reports attacking his wife. Then it was bye-bye Muskie" (Barnard, 1998).

Most caring mothers help their sons to be responsive to these cultural norms. They want to protect their sons from being perceived as weak. They don't want their sons to be victims of epithets that refer to closeness and femininity, such as "mama's boy" and "sissy" (Real, 1997). The fathers in our focus group also hold their sons at arm's length and eliminate any "demonstrations of physical affection," and they encourage their sons to be autonomous and to "make independent decisions." They fear the societal consequences of raising dependent sons, and several

According to Joseph Pleck, a principal investigator in the National Survey of Adolescent Males, "The more traditional the attitude about masculinity in adolescent males, the higher their risk for risky sexual behavior, substance use, educational problems and problems with the law."
—*Stephen Hall, "The Bully in the Mirror"*

To be an outcast boy is to be a "nonboy," to be feminine, to be weak.
—*Adrian Nicole LeBlanc, "The Outsiders"*

fathers affirmed a story told in one of the focus groups. This father said that he was warned by his neighbor not to be so physically affectionate with his young son because the child could grow up to be weak.

Many mothers want to help their children to avoid foreseeable mistakes. But fathers discussed how they want their sons to make their own mistakes and take the consequences. Mothers want to stop their children from being hurt. Mothers tend to express this need to protect by interceding on their child's behalf. One mother commented, "I don't buy the concept that you have to fail to succeed. I think you have to make mistakes, important mistakes, and learn from those mistakes. I think all you learn from failure is failure." We see the differences in the above statement between a mistake and a failure. A mistake is a misjudgment. A failure is the inability to meet our expectation, thus "falling short." Failures are internalized and often affect self-esteem. Boys perceive the decision by their fathers not to interfere as withdrawal and lack of interest. The mothers told us that they understand what their husbands are doing, but they can also see the need to clarify this reaction for their sons. Mothers often find themselves explaining their husbands to their sons.

The mothers with whom we spoke agreed that they would prefer to be proactive rather than reactive to situations. One of the mothers shared advice she had given to both her daughter and her son to minimize the number of unbearable consequences they would face. She constantly reinforced listening to their inner voice, adding, "Whenever they were in a situation where a decision had to be made, if their anchor seemed off-kilter, they needed to pay attention to that feeling." She always reinforced the idea, without having to know the particulars, that "their inner voice was telling them what was right or wrong." However, without an emotional vocabulary many boys can't find this anchor. When they're not in touch with their emotions, boys often do things for reasons that they're not aware of.

To the majority of gang members, the gang functions as an extension of — even a substitute for — the family. —Lonnie Jackson, Gangbusters: Strategies for Prevention and Intervention

This phenomenon is expressed throughout our culture, and influences the socially acceptable behaviors available for boys. For example, while the idea of being a tomboy is now an outmoded concept for girls, the boundaries for boys remain rigid (Sadker and Sadker, 1994). Boys work hard to purge themselves of any hint of softness or femininity. One mother tells how her sister made her promise not to give her son ballet lessons. When she told this story to her adolescent son, he said, "Thank God." When we asked boys in a focus group about name-calling, the majority agreed the worst name to be called during a verbal argument was "bitch."

It's no wonder then that males grow up more attuned to and comfortable with combat. Boys learn that the fastest way to resolve conflict may be a kick or a punch (Sadker and Sadker, 1994). When girls feel rejected or are made fun of, they tend to feel ashamed and internalize this feeling. Boys externalize this same feeling into anger. The boys in our focus groups agreed that "fighting somebody" was an acceptable way to resolve an argument. This perception even applies to the President of the United States. Colgate Professor Caroline Keating, a psychologist who specializes in studies of "leadership and deception," has found that, "When it comes to dominance among primates, the appearance of strength, the illusion of strength means more to us than anything else, maybe even more than the appearance of honesty. We can't admit to having a leader who's 'weak'" (Clines, 1998). Violence becomes a way of showing strength and dominance, while empathy and caring are seen as weaknesses and are discarded.

Gangs have become alternative families for some children by providing them with a sense of connection and identity. Gangs are one of the results of poverty, discrimination, and urban deterioration. The primary age of gang members is 14 to 20, with the average age around 18. Loyalty to a gang creates a sense of pride for members and a sense of being somebody. One gang member reports, "Yep. You know, like that old sayin', misery loves company? They was my homeboys 'cause we all thought the same and did the same thing." Boys who feel disenfranchised may be attracted to a gang. Another gang member said that being a member of a gang "made me [him] feel, ya know, powerful." Being part of a gang allows an adolescent to achieve a level of status not possible outside the gang culture (Jackson, 1998).

Despite their high profile in the media, relatively few boys join gangs. In fact, it has been reported that less than two percent of all juvenile crime is gang-related (Bodinger-deUriarte, 1993). Even though these numbers may be low, gangs have a powerful impact on teenagers because they play a significant role in the widespread increase of violence in schools (Burnett and Walz, 1994).

COULD A GANG ATTRACT YOUR SON?

Gang Checklist

Does your son evidence a sense of alienation and powerlessness?

Does he seek support outside traditional institutions?

Does your son search for love, structure, and discipline?

Does your son suffer from a lack of self-worth and status?

Does he seek a place of acceptance?

Does your son need physical safety and protection?

If you answer yes to a majority of these questions, you need to actively communicate with your son and monitor his behavior. This is another situation where it may be important to seek help from other adults in your son's life, his school, or a mental health professional.

While studying the roots of violence, we realized that emotional language and its expression are absent from many boys' lives. When emotional expression is absent, hostility and impulsive behavior appear.

Somewhere Between Superhero and Geek
How Do We Make It Okay for Boys to Break Out of the Box?

The American culture of masculinity is dominated by media images of violence that romanticize macho behavior. Our sons are relentlessly bombarded with these cultural messages. In the *Wall Street Journal,* Peggy Noonan (1999) calls the constant barrage of violent images a "culture of death." Noonan describes this culture of death as an ocean through which our children must swim. She writes, "Waves of sound and light, of thought and fact, come invisible through that water, like radar; they go through him again and again, from this direction and that. The sound from the television is a wave, and the sound from the radio; the headlines on the newsstand, on the magazines, on the ad on the bus as it whizzes by — all are waves." It's difficult enough for a boy with a mature understanding of who he is to filter out these cultural messages. Imagine how the typical boy struggling to find his identity is affected by this assault. These persistent messages propel boys to play a role defined by popular culture that often masks their fear and confusion. The result is that boys start to avoid opportunities to connect in a manner that helps them to address these feelings.

In our society, it is assumed that girls become women automatically, but boys are born amorphous and need to attain manhood. The process of attaining manhood is rigidly defined, and the acceptable avenues for boys are limited. In studying masculinity, one author concluded, "The boyhood development of masculine identity and status is truly problematic in a society that offers no official rite of passage into adulthood" (Messner, 1990). Rites of passage and rituals could provide boys with a greater sense of self-worth, connections to a spiritual life, greater knowledge of their own culture and history, and the encouragement to cultivate a sense of community (Tukufu, 1997).

The permissible avenues available for attaining masculinity are mostly contests that determine winners and losers. Few positive applications of this form of development exist for teenage boys other than sports. Common negative demonstrations of these contests are best exemplified by street violence, domestic violence, and fighting battles. Such behaviors have a profound effect on how boys affiliate and form friendships. It's not surprising that in high schools across the country, athletes attain the highest status. In the Littleton, Colorado, tragedy, the young killers targeted athletes because they felt put down by those boys' exalted position.

Even though men may be just as emotional and relational as women, they have been taught to exchange these qualities for athletic accomplishments and other achievements. For example, author Michael Gurian (1998) states, "By the time I had become a young man, I did not know what being brave, truthful, and good looked like. Nor did most young people. War — the great initiator of young men — had become a place not of bravery but of shame." These are certainly the words of someone who has never seen battle. Images from movies such as *Saving Private Ryan* and *The Thin Red Line,* as well as oral histories of the men who fought in World War II, the Korean War, and the Vietnam War don't create nostalgia. In fact, they evoke just the opposite. After listening to the voices of the men and women who returned from war, we created a new psychiatric category, post-traumatic stress disorder (PTSD), which validates the enormous distress that people experience when they witness horror, threat, or feel intense fear. Our goal is to guide parents and educators as they assist boys to define bravery, truth, and good in a manner that doesn't put them in danger.

Music has given voice to the current trauma that many teenagers experience daily. The following lyrics show this trauma at work.

The attraction to combativeness is demonstrated early in a boy's life. One focus group mother remembered the moment she decided it was okay to buy toy swords and other assorted weapons for her toddler son. She was driving with her son strapped in his car seat in the back seat. She handed him a peanut butter sandwich to eat during the drive. He took two or three bites and then stopped eating. "Pow, pow!" he yelled as he held the bread in his little fist and pointed it at the back of her head. She always cut the sandwich on the diagonal. With just a few bites, he had

Nightmares of bein' gunned down by fast foes

Shows no escape, I awake before my fate

Take precaution, when walkin' the streets I can't slumber

Knowin' somewhere lies a bullet with my number

Paranoid, can't avoid, what my life is due

My mind is strapped, monitored as ICU

Flashes of purses, I'm runnin' wild, hearin' nurses

Conversin' my mental state with my Old Earth

and I can't assure, here baby boy's gonna be fine

Stuck in a coma, only speakin' with one mind

The dream reoccurs, no sight of my assassins

in this mug, bloody visions of a gat and a slug

Schemin' for cream, in a reality it seems

to be my mind, duckin' death, in that land of dreams

—*Buddha Monk, "Land of My Dreams"*

fashioned himself an ingenious toy gun. The mothers in the focus groups all agreed that they didn't need to take these experiences away from young boys, but that they should teach responsibility and consequences of violence and aggressive behavior. These mothers were motivated to help their sons distinguish between fantasy, play, and reality. However, our culture and the media make this difficult.

A review of how "appropriate" maleness is presented in the media today demonstrates that little has changed in the last 25 years, except for the added pressure on boys to conform to a new image of masculine beauty. This pressure appears in mainstream advertising, where the image of the male ideal has become that of a muscular body with "six packs." One father, who is a long-distance runner and was preparing for a marathon, recalled walking into a natural food store for some

GENDER AND RACE BIAS IN THE MEDIA

Use the following exercise to increase your awareness of media biases. This type of exercise serves as a wonderful way to start a discussion with your son about his opinions of the media and how media images affect him. If you have difficulty making your lists from memory, start watching for examples during your everyday experiences with the media, including television, movies, magazines, and music. The goal is to realize how media creates stereotypes and to offer opportunities for dialogue between you and your son.

1. List three television shows or movies that portray what you consider to be positive role models.

Of Men	Of Women	Of People of Color
1.		
2.		
3.		

2. List three television shows or movies that portray what you consider to be negative role models.

Of Men	Of Women	Of People of Color
1.		
2.		
3.		

3. Name one television program, movie, video game, and song in which characters are portrayed in a stereotypical manner.

Television program	Movie	Video game	Song

4. List three magazines targeted for a particular audience. As you look through magazines, pay particular attention to the types of advertisements included to see what messages are being sent.

Male	Female	Male/Female	People of Color
1.			
2.			
3.			

carbohydrate powder. All he could find was protein, protein, and more protein. He observed that everything is currently aimed at building muscles.

A mother in one of our groups joked that her childhood image of masculinity did not include muscles. In fact, her only exposure to muscles was in advertisements of a muscular boy/man at the beach kicking sand in the face of a skinny boy. This image was usually in the back of magazines, with Charles Atlas selling some form of body-building aid.

Tormented by an unattainable ideal, boys are learning what girls have long known: it isn't easy living in a "Baywatch" world. *— Stephen Hall, "The Bully in the Mirror"*

Now, not only girls, but boys as well, must conform to a standard of beauty that exaggerates their maleness, using drugs, dietary additives, and extreme forms of exercise to attain this aesthetic ideal. We find ourselves asking, what happens to boys who can't attain this standard of masculine beauty? They, like girls, exhibit signs of image disturbances such as bulimia or "bigorexia" (compulsive body building) and steroid use (Bordo, 1999). A high school nurse for 25 years noticed a change in who came into her office to use the scale. She said, "At first, it was nearly all girls who wanted to weigh less. Then about 10 years ago, it quickly became mostly boys who wanted to bulk up. The pressure on girls to be slim was strong but subtle. The pressure on the boys, though, was overt:

Creatine, clinically proven strength, muscle function and energy enhancement for the best shape of your life. *—Advertisement for Creatine*

The pressure on boys to become large begins at an early age, as evidenced by the extreme bulking up of male action figures. For example, G.I. Joe dolls have increased in size every decade, beginning with the 1960s. When adjusted for scale, G.I. Joe's biceps grew from 12.2 inches in 1964 to 26.8 inches in 1998. As a reference, Mark McGwire, a large man with huge arms, has a bicep size of 20 inches, nearly seven inches short of the new "ideal." *—Jackson Katz, Tough Guise: Violence, Media, and the Crisis in Masculinity*

supervised, encouraged and, at times, required by their athletic coaches, as the other boys cheered on greater exhibitions of strength" (O'Connor, 1999). In reality, the pressure to become muscular begins even earlier, as evidenced by the extreme bulking up of male action figures. These popular toys, including G.I. Joe and Star Wars characters, have increased in size every decade since the 1960s; such subtleties can begin to exert size pressure on boys at a young age (Katz, 1999).

> The issue is not just violence in the media but the construction of violent masculinity as a cultural norm. From rock and rap music and videos, Hollywood action films, professional and college sports, the culture produces a stream of images of violent, abusive men and promotes characteristics such as dominance, power, and control as means of establishing or maintaining manhood. —*Jackson Katz and Sut Jhally, "The National Conversation in the Wake of Littleton is Missing the Mark"*

The shield of false bravado and toughness promoted in the media may lead to isolation and distance, as we have seen in the ways boys cope with sadness and problems (Pollack, 1998). The most popular male character types on television, in film, and in sports are still those with great physical strength who exhibit aggression and unequaled bravery, including gangster rap stars, action movie heroes, wrestlers, and characters in video games. Violent behavior for men, including its rewards, is encoded into our consciousness through mainstream advertising that uses common themes such as "acting out exhibits bravery," "strength is power," and "attitude is everything." The message is that cool is defined by being tough and rebellious and these are seen as desirable male traits.

Other popular themes in advertising depict uniformed soldiers and sports figures, complete with weapons and athletic gear, targeting young boys and adolescent males. The message here is that violence is cool and acceptable. What our kids are left with, even in the aftermath of disasters and violent massacres, "is a vicious cycle where even the examination of a disaster reinforces the violence-obsessed culture that may have helped trigger it. How can we remove the threads of violence from a society when those strands are so deeply woven into our character? We're left with a bromide: make sure that your kids don't get in so deep that fantasies cross over to the horrible, heartbreaking reality" (Levy, 1999).

There are alternatives to these limiting stereotypical role models, such as the baseball heroes of the 1998 season, Mark McGwire and Sammy Sosa. Mark McGwire even goes so far as to admit that "he could not have broken the long-ball record if he had not turned introspectively to therapists after a bad year at the plate" (Clines, 1998). McGwire also cried openly when he discussed his funding of a program for abused children. Sosa sent a message to his family after each home run.

Another potential source of positive media messages is through television sitcoms and dramas. Television shows often depict heroism and non-verbal warmth between characters, but very seldom do we see complicated inner feelings expressed between male friends like we do in episodes of the medical drama, ER.

> **Like his dad before him, Mark McGwire long suffered in silence. Not until he allowed his emotions to show and his tears to flow did he become what he really wanted to be.** —*Rick Reilly, "The Good Father"*

When Doug Ross's (played by George Clooney) father died, Doug planned to travel alone to scatter his father's ashes. While he made it very clear that he could do this alone, his friend, Mark Green (played by Anthony Edwards), insisted on accompanying him. As the episode unfolds, each friend shares his experiences and feelings while validating how different, yet conflicted the other's relationship was with his father. At the end of the segment, Doug is openly grateful that his friend accompanied him, and both characters have clearly benefitted from and valued the experience of being together. Teenage boys could benefit from seeing more stories about such shared experiences. Stories with other emotionally complex themes, human connections, and feelings are needed in television, movies, and other media. We are encouraged by new avenues for connection that are being forged on the

Internet. For example, stay-at-home dads have several sites they can chat in and provide support for one another (Marin, 2000). However, we're concerned about the boys who have Mark McGwire's depth of feeling, but who don't conform to traditional masculine ideals. This boy is best depicted in the following poem:

I Knew This Kid

I knew this skinny little kid
        Who never wanted to play tackle football at all
But thought he'd better if he wanted
        his daddy to love him and to prove his courage
and things like that.
        I remember him holding his breath
And closing his eyes
        And throwing a block into a guy twice his size.
Proving he was brave enough to be loved, and crying softly
        Because his tailbone hurt
And his shoes were so big they made him stumble.

I knew this skinny little kid
        With sky-blue eyes and soft brown hair
Who liked cattails and pussy willows.
        Sumac huts and sassafras,
Who liked chestnuts and pine cones and oily walnuts,
        Lurking foxes and rabbits munching lilies,
Secret caves and moss around the roots of oaks,
        Beavers and muskrats and gawking herons.
And I wonder what he would have been
        If someone had loved him for
Just following the fawns and building waterfalls
        And watching the white rats have babies.
I wonder what he would have been
        If he hadn't played tackle football at all.

        —James Kavanaugh

The Debate About Nature Versus Nurture
How Powerful Is Biology and Its Impact on Behavior and Learning?

The question of nature versus nurture has been much debated during the 20th century. It is usually framed as a dialectic, pitting biology against culture and heredity against environment. In fact, the debate has again gone to extremes with Judith Rich Harris's recent book, *The Nurture Assumption* (1998), which theorizes that a child's peer group has more influence on his or her development than the child's family. We believe this debate has created a false and unproductive conflict. There is little practical utility to choosing between nurture and nature. A more productive inquiry would be to understand how heredity and environment interact to impact developing human behavior. This interplay of biology and sociology exists in a conjoint relationship, "the one always already contains the other." Even though biology affects culture, it can't be isolated from culture to be studied as an independent variable (Segal, 1990).

One scientist hypothesized, "Part of the brain is hard-wired in advance of birth and part of the brain, like clay, is malleable through experience" (Gutkind, 1993). The intertwined relationship of biology and environment can be understood by looking at our historical past. "During our fathers', grandfathers', and great grandfathers' generations, men and their dependents were better off if they weren't too emotionally

> The belief that violence is manly is not carried on any chromosome, not soldered into the wiring of the right or left hemisphere, not juiced by testosterone. (Half of all boys don't fight, most don't carry weapons, and almost all don't kill: are they not boys?) Boys learn it. Violence, Dr. [Carol] Gilligan writes, "has far more to do with the cultural construction of manhood than it does with the hormonal substrates of biology."
> —*Michael Kimmel, "What Are Little Boys Made Of?"*

inclined" (Levant, 1995). Men needed focus, almost tunnel vision to withstand long hours of work to provide food and shelter for their families. Sensitivity and self-awareness would have compromised their ability to filter out stimuli and stay focused. Looking out for family was all-consuming for most men and required them to harden themselves against emotionality. However, just as we no longer need our appendix, an argument can be made that men cutting off their emotions no longer protects their family, or themselves, very well. Our environment and culture have changed in some ways but haven't adapted in other ways.

Unlike much of the rest of the world, Americans do not prefer boys. Of the first microsort (a procedure that allows parents to choose a baby's sex by sorting sperm) attempts, 83 were for girls.
—*Lisa Belkin, "Getting the Girl"*

Infant boys are cuddled, talked to, and breast fed for significantly shorter periods of time than infant girls.
—*Michael Gurian, A Fine Young Man*

Research shows that biological differences in the brain function of males and females do exist; recently the scientific community has been more willing to admit this. Diane Halpern, a psychology professor at California State University in San Bernardino, reviewed recent research on the differences between male and female intelligence. She found that women perform better in tasks that test language abilities, fine motor skills, perceptual speed, decoding nonverbal communication, and speech articulation. On the other hand, men do better in visual working memory, tasks that require moving objects, aiming, fluid reasoning, knowledge of math, science, and geography, and general knowledge. In addition, she found that female brains are oriented to the left hemisphere, where language is processed, while male brains are stronger in the right hemisphere, the spatial and physical center. Furthermore, research in brain study has shown that the two hemispheres are better connected in females (Rosenfeld, 1998).

Nevertheless, Michael Reichert, project director of "On Behalf of Boys," at The Haverford School for Boys in Haverford, Pennsylvania, believes that biological differences between boys and girls are exaggerated and magnified by the prevailing culture. For example, Reichert states: "Schools have traditionally been complicit in making boys believe that what they feel inside is not as important as what they do. We turn them into totally instrumental beings, prepared for work and soldiering" (Sokolove, 1997). We argue that a better way of examining the impact of biological differences between the sexes is to do so holistically. Using current brain science, combined with psychological developmental theories, new knowledge is helping parents understand boys holistically, rather than focusing only on their aggressive characteristics. Thus, the varying ways that parents relate to their children produces different brains and, consequently, different behaviors (Begley, 1995).

According to Terrence Real (1997), "Boys and men are fundamentally just as relational as girls and women." It isn't that men have fewer relational needs than women; they've been conditioned to filter those needs through the screen of achievement. We need to widen the scope of acceptable behavior for boys to give them other options besides aggressive, competitive, and emotionally constricted outlets. We believe the goal is not to take away from, but rather to extend the options available to, all boys and girls. In this way, parents can take into consideration the needs of individual boys and girls, instead of grouping them according to gender. As Susan Bailey, executive director of the Wellesley Center for Women, concluded, "There is no one-size-fits-all solution for either girls or boys" (Hornblower, 1998).

There are many misconceptions about the biology of boyhood. Testosterone alone doesn't determine the way boys are. "Boys do play differently than girls, but their style of play is not solely a function of testosterone and it certainly does not prove a proclivity for violence" (Pollack, 1998). Testosterone may explain the amount of energy a boy exhibits, but his behavior may be better explained by how he is loved. Indeed, Pollack states, it is the influence of mothering, fathering, and love on boyhood that is just as much a part of his development as nature. As parents, we can influence the pro-social expression of this energy. Our influence as parents is very profound. In fact, some of the newest research on the interplay of violence and biology in the book *The Biology of Violence,* finds that "Behavior is the result of a dialogue between your brain and your experiences" (Niehoff, 1999). Children's brains are very pliable, and are not exclusively programmed at birth. Parents can actually affect the circuitry in their little boys' brains.

Each experience in a young child's life leads to new neurological connections. Even if one believes that boys are born more aggressive than girls, aggression doesn't have to be the defining characteristic of a boy. Nurturing affects a child's neurological connections and creates opportunities for a boy to attain emotional intelligence. Boys will benefit from parental help and permission in developing their capacity for empathy and attachment. This can be accomplished if parents understand that it's in a boy's best interests to keep a close connection with his parents. As parents, we have to intentionally teach the language of empathy and nurturing skills while a son grows up. One parent explained how she connects with her son: "I understand his nonverbal expressions, and when I think he needs to express himself I purposefully engage him in general conversation, usually while cooking dinner. After awhile, he feels comfortable enough to tell me what's on his mind." Her son doesn't know her intentions, but what he feels is his mother's ability to be with him. These interactions build and sustain human closeness and connections.

We want to emphasize that while there are differences between males and females, this knowledge shouldn't foster more stereotypes about the aggressive and destructive aspects of male behavior. Actually, the "knowledge of the evolution of brain differences teaches us that societies are capable of creating intimate and fruitful human relationships that

Testosterone may explain the amount of energy a boy exhibits but his behavior may be better explained by how he is loved.

— *William Pollack, Real Boys: Rescuing Our Sons from the Myths of Boyhood*

Boys are perceived and nurtured differently than girls, even before they leave the womb. Though there is no measurable difference between boy and girl fetal-activity levels, mothers carrying boys "routinely describe the babies' movements as vigorous, earthquake-like, very strong and girls' as very gentle."

— *Ross Parke and Armin Brott, Throwaway Dads*

nurture both the best of the female and best of the male brains. Our mistake is not in letting 'boys be boys'; it's in letting boys be boys without the proper care, love and discipline" (Gurian, 1998).

Although current research focuses on documenting the differences between genders, we must remember that within each gender is diversity. These differences are especially evident in the ways children learn. Parents shouldn't make assumptions and impose expectations about what boys can and cannot do based exclusively on their "nature." One focus group parent talked about how difficult it was for her husband to accept the fact that their son was not a good athlete and to appreciate his interest in reading books and writing stories. Parents must give their child opportunities to strengthen less proficient areas and skills, while supporting their child's learning preferences.

Think about the ways in which your son learns best, and review the following information about learning strategies. Most likely your son is a composite of all three learning strengths, but one of them probably works best for him. However, one or more of these areas may be a real problem for him. Help him to identify and use his preferred style whenever he can.

HOW DOES YOUR SON LEARN BEST?

Learning Strengths
- If he learns best when he listens, he may be an auditory learner.
- If he learns best when he looks at something, he may be a visual learner.
- If he learns best by doing things, he may be a kinesthetic learner.

In addition to learning strengths, your son may prefer one type of learning over another. Review the following categories to further understand his learning preferences.

Learning Types
Field Independent
- Learning is abstract and analytical.
- Learning is not necessarily related to environment, experience, and personality.
- Learning is individual- and teacher-centered.

Field Sensitive
- Learning is related to environment, experience, and personality.
- Personal and social impact are important, as are practical values.
- Attention needs to be paid to contextual field.
- One is sensitive to personal dynamics and criticism.
- Learning is cooperative and group- or peer-centered.

Learning Styles
1. Read the descriptions of the four types of learning styles below.
2. Circle the one style that seems to fit your son best. (All of the styles may describe part of him, but pick the one that seems to be more like him than the others.)
3. Check the one style that seems to fit him the least.
4. Ask your son to do the same.

Sensing/Feeling Style
He likes or prefers to:
- Work with a friend or friends
- Share opinions with other students
- Think out loud with others
- Work in a relaxed environment
- Receive personal attention from the teacher
- Be shown what to do by another person
- Help other students learn
- Work as part of a team

Sensing/Thinking Style
He likes or prefers to:
- Put what he learns immediately into practice
- See results from his efforts right away

- Practice what he has learned
- Follow directions one step at a time
- Work in an organized environment
- Study about practical things
- Answer factual questions
- Do something rather than read about it
- Be active
- Have his work checked immediately
- Know exactly what is expected of him

Intuitive/Thinking Style
He likes or prefers to:
- Work independently and think for himself
- Plan and think through things before he begins to work
- Study about ideas and how things are related
- Read about things he wants to know
- Plan a project on his own
- Argue or debate a point
- Answer questions that require him to analyze and think logically
- Solve problems by collecting and organizing data
- Organize and give structure to things and ideas
- Study theories and ideas
- Gather data and information from different sources

Intuitive/Feeling Style
He likes or prefers to:
- Be creative and use his imagination
- Look for new ways to express himself
- Use a variety of resources
- Not have too many routines to follow
- Dream and fantasize about possibilities
- Follow his own interests
- Work on several things at one time
- Work at his own pace
- Look for new and unusual solutions to problems
- Express himself artistically

Compare what your son has told you about his learning preferences and how he works best with your own observations. Using this information only as a guide, try to encourage your son to lead with his strengths, while also trying to improve areas that he finds more challenging. You may want to share this information with your son's teachers.

There may not be such a thing as child development anymore. Instead, researchers are now studying each gender's development separately and discovering that boys and girls face very different sorts of challenges. Review the following developmental time line for more information.

Boys

0-3 years
At birth, boys have brains that are 5% larger than girls' (size doesn't affect intelligence) and proportionately larger bodies — disparities that increase with age.

4-6 years
The start of school is a tough time as boys must curb aggressive impulses. They lag behind girls in reading skills, and hyperactivity may be a problem.

7-10 years
While good at gross motor skills, boys trail girls in finer control. Many of the best students but also nearly all of the poorest ones are boys.

11-13 years
A mixed bag. Dropout rates begin to climb, but good students start pulling ahead of girls in math skills and catching up some in verbal ones.

14-16 years
Entering adolescence, boys hit another rough patch. Indulging in drugs, alcohol and aggressive behavior are common forms of rebellion.

Girls

0-3 years
Girls are born with a higher proportion of nerve cells to process information. More brain regions are involved in language production and recognition.

4-6 years
Girls are well suited to school. They are calm, get along with others, pick up on social cues, and reading and writing come easily to them.

7-10 years
Very good years for girls. On average, they outperform boys at school, excelling in verbal skills while holding their own in math.

11-13 years
The start of puberty and girls' most vulnerable time. Many experience depression; as many as 15% may try to kill themselves.

14-16 years
Eating disorders are a major concern. Although anorexia can manifest itself as early as 8, it typically afflicts girls starting at 11 or 12; bulimia at 15.

Chapter 10

Historical Perspective:
The Myth of the "Good Old Days"
Do We Want Things the Way They Were?

Overview

Every generation is told that their youth is more out of control and has more serious issues to deal with than past generations. Understanding history and the interplay of culture and psychology can tell us much about the dilemmas boys and parents face today. This insight can help us to create successful parenting strategies.

In the past, teenage boys had more opportunities to demonstrate their manhood than they do now, such as through more rigidly defined gender roles. Today, many of the rules no longer apply. While teenagers mature physically at an earlier age than ever before, their opportunity to gain economic independence arrives later than in the past. Teenagers now remain in high school until age 18, and may still be unable to support themselves when they graduate (Coontz, 1997). While high schools were originally created for the most privileged, a high school diploma no longer ensures a stable job that can support a family. Even a partial college education doesn't provide the same advantage that it used to. Therefore, "Adolescence has become a social and economic holding period," with parents doing the holding (Coontz, 1997).

> What many young people have lost are clear paths for gaining experience doing responsible, socially necessary work, either in or out of the home, and for moving away from parental supervision without losing contact with adults. —*Stephanie Coontz, The Way We Really Are: Coming to Terms with America's Changing Families*

The age at which our children can support themselves, let alone a family, has reached a new high in the last two decades. In fact, a report published by the American Youth Policy Forum (1998) demonstrates that the percentage of young adults living at home has increased in the last 25 years, and males, ages 20–29, are more likely than girls (42 percent versus 30 percent) to live in their parents' or other relatives' homes. Given this change in the economic reality, and the emergence of a different living pattern within families, we tend to yearn for the "good old days." This takes baby boomer parents back to the 1950s.

The Myth of the "Good Old Days"

Why does popular culture idealize the 1950s? Perhaps because the perception is that many people, mostly the majority culture, felt more confident in the '50s, and had an overriding sense of optimism. An average 30-year-old White man could buy a medium-priced house with 15–18 percent of his salary (Coontz, 1997). People formed and maintained families more predictably, and there was a coherent and strictly defined moral order. We sometimes remind teenagers of how much better things were in our idealized conception of the past. We romanticize our two-parent household with a stay-at-home mom and a father as the provider. This family configuration has provided the template for our sense of stability.

The model for the so-called ideal family was popularized and reinforced when mass media began to have a significant impact on society. The idea of the housewife began during the post-war period, when many women stayed at home and found their lives engulfed by domestic chores. These "ideal" women were depicted in dramas and sitcoms on television. The demographics of actual American families in the 1950s were different from our perception of the ideal model. For example, many African American women had to work outside the home to provide for their families. Furthermore, even those who lived the supposed ideal were not necessarily happy with it. Betty Friedan and others exposed the high incidence of depression in the 1950s and '60s and they showed the dark side of the picket fence dream, even for many of the privileged Whites who appeared to be living it (Friedan, 1997).

The '50s housewife could be said to have morphed into the '90s man. The empty compensations of a "feminine mystique" are transforming into the empty compensations of a masculine mystique, with a gentlemen's cigar club no more satisfying than a ladies' bake-off.
—Susan Faludi, "The Betrayal of the American Man"

Currently, there is not just one type of family, but there never really was just one type of family. The White, middle-class families portrayed on *Ozzie and Harriet, Father Knows Best, Leave it to Beaver,* and *Donna Reed* represent a myth that remains with us today. In fact, the real Harriet Nelson was a working actress who co-produced her own television show.

What We Can Learn from Single Parents

One of the new realities of contemporary life is the large number of children being raised by single parents. It's common knowledge that raising a child alone can be difficult. However, let's dispel some of the assumptions about whether a single parent can raise a son successfully. We don't want to romanticize the challenges of raising children alone, but we do want to demonstrate that a child can flourish in a single parent home. All parents can learn from the resilience of single parents who have successfully raised competent sons.

Single parent families comprise a significant percentage of American households. The U.S. Census Report estimates that single parent families account for 27 percent of the total number of families with children, a proportion that has been increasing rapidly over the last few years (Cohn, 1998). A comparison of single parent households by race/ethnicity indicates that this type of family is even more prevalent among communities of color. In 1998, 51 percent of African American families were headed by single mothers, and 4 percent by single fathers; 27 percent of Latino families were headed by single mothers, and 4 percent by single fathers; and 18 percent of White families were headed by single mothers, and 5 percent by single fathers (Federal Interagency Forum on Child and Family Statistics, 1999). Given the tremendous increase in the numbers of single parent families, we need to address the specific needs of this family configuration.

About 13.5 million American children live with a single parent who is working, new Census Bureau data show. This includes 10.9 million living with working moms and 2.6 million living with working dads. In 1998, 19.7 million of the 71.4 million American children lived with only one parent, including 16.6 million who lived with their mother and 3.1 million who lived with their father. Of those, 5.7 million lived with a single mom and 0.5 million with a single dad who was unemployed or not in the labor force. The median income for single parents with children is $12,064 for a never-married mother, $21,316 for a divorced mother, and $32,968 for a divorced father. This compares with a median income for two-parent households of $52,553. — *U. S. Census Bureau, "Children With Single Parents: How They Fare"*

Rather than lamenting the absence of a parent, we need to focus on what the child has and needs. One communicative and emotionally intelligent parent can be more than just adequate. An engaged parent can cultivate a positive and strong relationship that promotes growth and helps a child realize his or her maximum potential. The single parent experience provides growth opportunities for both the parent and the child. Boys in our focus groups from single parent households reported feeling both connected to their mothers and competent because of the responsibility they, the boys, assume within their households. In addition, single parents in the focus groups reported that raising a child alone provided them with a feeling of competence they had not felt before.

A single parent raising a child of the opposite sex needs to expand his or her role. For example, the single mother raising a son needs to understand more fully the inner life of a boy because she might not be able to share some of these responsibilities with his father. These experiences can be enriching and can lead to personal growth for the parent. One of the advantages for boys raised in households with single mothers is that they may not be as fearful of relationships. These boys aren't as closely bound to patriarchal stereotypes and are better prepared emotionally for satisfying relationships with men and women (Walters, 1998).

Other positive findings about boys raised with single mothers include:

- These boys have more permission to form their sense of self with less reliance on stereotypes, such as, "Be tough," "Stop hanging around with mom," or "Don't be a sissy" (Engber and Klungness, 1995).

- Boys raised by single mothers tend to have better relationships with women later in life (Engber and Klungness, 1995).

While it's statistically true that the vast majority of these single parent families are headed by women (16.6 million), the number of households headed by fathers has grown from 1.7 million to 3.1 million (Cohn, 1998). This cultural shift heightens the necessity to prepare boys for the childcare roles more of them will undertake. Boys need skills that will enhance their parenting success. As one single father stated in *The Washington Post*, "Many men feel uncomfortable talking about personal matters, including child-rearing problems, and thus suffer in silence. Fathers tend to be isolated and don't know how to approach other fathers about parenting issues, whereas mothers are very good at that" (Cohn, 1998).

It is becoming clearer every day that more men are being held accountable for childcare, in both two-parent and single parent households. One indication of this comes from an observation by a nurse in the maternity ward of a Maryland hospital. She noted that the involvement of fathers in the delivery process had increased greatly during her 30-year career. We believe this involvement indicates greater interest by men in increasing their roles as fathers. This finding is evidence of the need for young men to build more parenting skills. Learning to communicate and acquiring skills when boys are young will give them the tools they need and access to a community of other parents.

In general, whether headed by a single mother or a single father, single parent families have strengths that aren't usually discussed, such as a single line of authority that simplifies family decision-making (Walters, 1998). For example, very often parents disagree about rules for teenagers. In a single parent family, the child knows that there is only one set of rules, with only one interpretation, and less opportunity for skilled negotiation. For example, a midnight curfew is a midnight curfew.

Single parent families also call for one parent to combine both the managerial and nurturing functions (Walters, 1998). This is a beneficial model for a child, regardless of whether the single parent is a mother or father. Boys and girls benefit from seeing their mothers as household head and nurturer. Similarly, they benefit from receiving nurturing from their father and from his role as family manager. In addition, single parent families have less of a hierarchy regarding household tasks, which fosters greater sharing of family jobs (Walters, 1998). A single parent can't do it all alone and will more commonly accept and encourage participation from the children. In a two-parent home, the child might not be expected to help or might be able to get away with not doing chores. This sharing of responsibility contributes to the child's self-esteem.

Children benefit from the opportunity to make contributions to the family. They know that they have something to offer that the parent values, and in return, they feel a sense of independence and accomplishment. Chores are confidence builders and become the child's first step toward self-reliance (Walters, 1998). The children in these families are more confident that they have something else to offer their parent, besides staying out of trouble and getting good grades. There are also more opportunities for a child to nurture his or her parent. While there is a danger in treating the child like an adult, or as it is described in the mental health field, "parentified child," many children benefit from the heightened sense of competence that comes from just knowing they can help (Walters, 1998). You may want to use the following list of chores to see who is doing what in your household.

It is difficult to get children to do chores, but it may help you to remember that chores provide opportunities for family participation and for building children's self-worth.

CHECKLIST: WHO'S DOING THE CHORES?

List of Chores	Who	Day(s)
1. Taking out the garbage		
2. Loading dishwasher		
3. Unloading dishwasher		
4. Raking leaves		
5. Mowing lawn		
6. Vacuuming		
7. Dusting		
8. Mopping		
9. Laundry (loading or folding)		
10. Helping to prepare for meals (e.g., setting table or cooking)		
11. Tidying one's own room		
12. Washing the car		
13. Feeding/walking pets		
14. Babysitting younger siblings		

Parents and families can learn a lot from studying single parent families. For example, just as we learned that we have to train our girls for outside work and housework, it's also not enough to train boys only for work outside the home. Behavior and communication skills that are adequate in the world of work are inadequate in the world of families. Our goal as parents should be to help our boys learn "outside the home skills" and "inside the home skills," not only for themselves, but for their future relationships and children. This need requires us to encourage our boys to talk. They need to be taught the lessons of emotional intelligence and to articulate self-expression.

- Do expect that most boys grow and mature at a slower rate than girls, so be patient about your son's development.

- Do teach your son values but let him express them in his own masculine way, which may mean not showing his feelings about things the way you do.

- Don't worry that he won't learn manly things without a man at home. Half the population is male, and he is certain to pick up social skills from other males he comes in contact with.

- Do believe in yourself and try to encourage self- esteem in your child as well. Let your child know that you are confident as a parent.

- Don't avoid talking about his father even if you didn't know him well. Give your son someone to think about with whom he can identify. Point out positive traits your son may possess that remind you of his father.

- Do teach your son to show respect for both males and females and to cultivate friendships with both.

- Don't ever make your son the "man of the house." He can have responsibilities and chores, but they shouldn't be representative of what is expected of grown men.

- Do help him seek healthy male role models. Point out the positive qualities in men you see on a day-to-day basis, including the helpful shoe salesman, the friendly pharmacist, or the talkative neighborhood patrolman.

- Do limit the amount of violence your son witnesses. Let him know that what is shown on television is not always the way healthy men should behave.

Reprinted with permission from Andrea Engber and Leah Klungness, Ph.D. The Complete Single Mother ©1995, Andrea Engber and Leah Klungness. Published by Adams Media Corporation.

Today's Challenges

Life may be more challenging today, not necessarily because of new family configurations, but because teenagers have such high expectations of what life should bring, little ability to delay gratification, more exposure to danger, and fewer avenues to substantive work (Palladino, 1996). It's probably true that in the past teenagers had less trouble making decisions, because they had fewer choices to make. Moreover, some of our population, such as middle-class White males, can't expect the kind of privileges they could count on in the past, as Latino, African American, and Asian American males and females continue to make progress toward taking their rightful place in society. Further, the computer age has made youth more suspicious of adults as guides on the path to maturity because those very adults seem more confused than their own children by the technological revolution.

It is also true that adolescence, although historically defined by risky behavior, has become even more dangerous for children. The expected experimentation and risks have become life-threatening. Sex, since AIDS, is deadly to many. The proliferation of weapons in the hands of young people has escalated the street fight of the past into a deadly demonstration of firepower today. This new reality creates anxieties in adults that are different from those in the past. Parents fear, justifiably, that if a teenager makes a mistake, it could be fatal.

Many of these conflicts between adult fears and teen behavior are triggered by the changes in our society's economic and social arrangements. Currently, boys at the bottom of the pyramid use different strategies to cope — turning inward or outward, sometimes in highly destructive ways. There has been a fivefold jump in the homicide and suicide rates of boys in the last 40 years, a rise some experts attribute to increasing male depression and anger as well as access to guns, among other factors (LeBlanc, 1999). While the boys in our focus groups don't see themselves as being vulnerable, focus group parents express

> The world has changed so much around us that what our parents did is no longer enough. There have always been kids on the edge. Increasingly, there are forces conspiring to push them over.
>
> —*Lisa Belkin, "Parents Blaming Parents"*

concern about their sons being targets of other boys' anger and alienation. Parents are acutely aware that their sons are at greater risk; as one mother said, "Keeping my son safe is my top priority. Until my son comes home at night, I can't fall asleep."

The mythical view of our past is very compelling. However, we need to keep a realistic perspective about the differences between the past and the present. For instance, regardless of the spin that parents and teachers put on the "good old days," the past worked better for White men and boys than for women and people of color. Women had fewer options, people of color "knew their place," and our culture offered one homogenized White image of female beauty and male privilege. Indeed, the civil rights and the women's movements began in response to the social and economic inequities of the times. With this in mind, we believe that both the "good old days" and these days have positive and negative qualities. We hope to learn lessons from the past, while focusing our energies toward alleviating the problems of today.

Strategies for Parents: A Baker's Dozen
Where Do We Go from Here?

A dolescent boys are forced to grow up experiencing a "relational paradox" or double bind. Boys experience emotional connections, but, at the same time, are told to conceal their need for them. For this reason, we have to intentionally teach and model connection. Every family has operating principles and values that are unique to it and will affect what works and what doesn't. Be confident in teaching those principles and values that are specific to your culture and heritage. Keep in mind that suggested strategies that work sometimes, may not work at other times, or for every family.

Parents won't know what will work in advance. However, by trying, parents will become more knowledgeable, indeed more artful, about what works for their son. Even with those strategies that do work, flexibility, variety, and a sense of humor are critical to getting through these turbulent years. Anyone who says these years are easy has never lived or worked with a teenage boy. However, we believe that these years are also filled with wonder, tenderness, and opportunities for personal growth for parents. These experiences and moments are to be treasured for those who stay involved, who stay connected.

Psychiatrist Dr. Stephen Bergman says, "All human beings have the same nature, which is to want to be in a good connection, and all you're doing with boys is to come back to what they experience as little boys and give them what they yearn for." —*Carey Goldberg, "Growing Move to Address a Cultural Threat to Boys"*

Strategies for Parents: A Baker's Dozen

1. Teach the language of feelings; empathy has to be taught and modeled in the home.

Label a feeling from an early age and interpret experiences from a feeling level to promote emotional intelligence. Teach the impact of behaviors and actions on others — for example, ask your son, "When you did that, how do you think I felt?"

Teach your boy to handle toughness and tenderness. Work to harness his energy in a way that includes his sweetness, vulnerability, loyalty and commitment, protectiveness, honor, and integrity. These are also genuine characteristics of boys.

Early on, mothers need to try to teach their sons empathy, and they need to mentor them on relational skills. Initially, you do this by talking about your own feelings and theirs. Your personal stories will reach your child in a way that lecturing never can. No one listens to a sermon.

Teach by example. Try to resolve disputes calmly and reasonably without yelling. Talk about the reality of their lives and your own personal experiences. Share with them your successes and your failures.

Share your feelings about the day, issues, and relationships. Discuss openly with your partner his or her feelings so children know it's okay to express feelings out loud.

I don't allow them to disappear into their own rooms all the time, I don't care how quiet or how separate they try to make themselves, you have to stay with them, you have to stay involved.

—*Focus Group Mother*

2. Place a value on staying attached in the way we do for our daughters.

Sons also need to feel connected to family, even if they do so on their own terms. The goal is to stay connected. Keep family time a part of his time.

Encourage sons to express their feelings; don't let them off the hook any more than you would a daughter. Apply the same standards of connectedness to a son as you would to a daughter. Tell your son how you, as parents, feel by using emotional language. Don't count your son out when you would count your daughter in. Expect him to attend family functions, even if he protests, because it helps to build closeness and a sense of family.

Give your son opportunities for time with his extended family members and friends, understanding that sometimes it's easier for him to stay connected with his own family through experiences with his extended family.

Let your son know that even if he chooses to separate for a period of time, he is always welcome to come back.

3. Trust your instincts about what you know is good for your son.

Don't succumb to the pressures of society to push your son away. He will not become a "wimp" if he is loved by and connected to his family and friends. In fact, his self-esteem is more likely to stay intact knowing that he is loved. Don't give away your authority as parents to teachers, coaches, or other parents.

Mothers must stay involved; they can't love their sons too much. Don't worry about

> If given a little more time, we could explore the significance of the word taming, but I think of "The Horse Whisperer" as opposed to those who break horses. We tend to stand the boys up and say, what did you do? We ought to take them on our laps and cuddle them, and that is what is meant by taming, the horse whisperer, rather than the breaking model. —*James Garbarino, Lost Boys: Why Our Sons Turn Violent and How We Can Save Them*

saying, "Drive carefully," every time they take the car. You care, and they do want to hear it.

If you are a single parent, believe in yourself as a strong and confident guide for your son. High self-esteem and a positive attitude can be contagious. Negative language, such as "broken home," should be replaced with language that reflects the value of a single parent home. Single parent households offer advantages, as well as challenges, to children's self-esteem.

Teach your sons to trust their own instincts, listen to their own internal voices. When their internal "anchor" feels out of sorts in response to certain situations or behavioral choices, teach them not to do whatever "it" is, until they can act in a manner that makes them feel good about themselves.

4. Avoid reinforcing negative stereotypes.

Interrupt the cycle of racism by teaching your son to be a "Bias Buster" (Derman-Sparks, 1989). Discuss with him all aspects of intolerance. Teach him how to recognize it and how to interrupt it for himself and for others. Beverly Daniel Tatum gives the following description of one method to eliminate intolerance. She suggests using the ABCs to teach:

A = Affirming identity
B = Building community
C = Cultivating leadership

If our sons are going to live successfully in a pluralistic society, we must teach them how to interrupt the cycle of intolerance.

Be mindful of your own biases to consciously increase your children's awareness of options. Give boys and girls experiences in and outside the home. When assigning household tasks, give boys and girls a variety of responsibilities. When planning after-school or summer experiences, base these decisions on the needs and passions of the individual child. Your children will need these experiences to become confident and emotionally responsive adults.

Increase ways for boys to affiliate, beyond what's encouraged by popular culture (e.g., music and sports). Introduce them to the value of participation in non-traditional activities (e.g., science, chess, and the arts). Show boys regularly why you value these activities and how you benefit from them.

Boys are taught that the worst thing to be is a sissy or a coward or a mama's boy. If we are ever going to raise a generation of males who grow into less violent men, then it seems to me we have to start challenging some of these stereotypes about masculinity. —*Dr. James Gilligan, Violence: Reflections on a National Epidemic*

Decide family activities based on interest, rather than gender. Encourage boys to try new things. Give them positive independent experiences such as camp, religious retreats, and visiting relatives.

Support the importance of maintaining relationships with girls as friends. Don't tease or sexualize boy/girl friendships. The boys in our focus groups were very clear about how essential their friendships with girls were. Girls give back to them what we ask boys to give up.

Raising boys to manhood means confronting racism, sexism, and homophobia — both in our communities and in ourselves. —*Paul Kivel, Boys Will Be Men: Raising Our Sons for Courage, Caring, and Community*

5. **Learn to find and use the teachable moment.**

It's impossible, if not counterproductive, to "be on" boys all of the time about these issues. Learn your son's signals; boys give more subtle cues than girls about when it is safe to approach them emotionally. This isn't easy, so don't be too hard on yourself if you miss the cues or approach your son in the wrong way. There will be other opportunities. When a boys bursts into a room ready to share some observations, whether it's a sports fact or something outrageous on Jerry Springer, understand that this may be his way of connecting and communicating. Be open to dialogue, even at odd hours.

> **Don't be accusing, just start talking, ease into sort of a general conversation.**
> *—Focus Group Mother*

React to what your son says without overwhelming him. Your son may be sensitive when you make a "big deal" about his communicating with you. Try not to make him feel too noticed or patronized. Remember that boys will do anything to avoid feeling shamed. Make sure that you don't criticize or patronize him for showing such emotions as sadness and fear. Never use language that makes him feel ashamed. Be vigilant about dealing with shaming messages that authority figures give to your son; for example, teach him how to cope with coaches who criticize their players for playing "like girls."

Try to answer his questions as honestly as possible, no matter how difficult or how uncomfortable they may make you feel. If he doesn't get the answers from you, he will certainly get them elsewhere. While he may still seek out and adopt his friends' views on the same matter, at least he can think about what you had told him.

> **What you see and what you read is indicative of what you do.** *—Focus Group Father*

Be involved with, or aware of, what your son is watching or listening to on the television, CD player, and computer. Discuss your feelings about violence in the media. Watch movies and television together and talk about what you observe or feel. Offer media alternatives that depict boys and men as caring and connected. Discuss the impact of the music they listen to and provide them with an alternate framework. Your son probably won't buy into your ideas at first; he may even appear to ignore you. Over time, however, he will likely integrate your views into his value system. But you'll probably be the last to know it.

6. **Give boys permission to feel bad.**

Look beneath their expressions of anger. Many times this emotion masks their inability to know that they are feeling sad.

Listen to your son's questions, complaints, and comments about peers, siblings, and adults, and make an effort to read between the lines to discover where the real problems, if any, may lie. Don't be too quick to react. Conflict provides a real opportunity to learn how he sees the world and what his life issues are.

Create an emotionally supportive atmosphere where it's alright to cry and it won't shame him.

Learn the signs of depression and take them seriously (see chart on page 35 and Appendix G). Don't be afraid to ask for help when tackling this problem.

7. **Set limits, even if he fights you.**

Firm, consistent, but not rigid limits make children feel safe. Children are supposed to challenge you, but you're still supposed to guide them. Don't abdicate your responsibility to watch over them and protect them. Expect to know where your sons are and have them check in with you, just as you would with your daughter, or as adults do with one another.

Set an age-appropriate curfew for your son and enforce it. Explain to him that he will eventually enjoy all the freedoms of an adult, but full and total freedom is not appropriate for a teenager.

Teach and expect responsible use of his car or the family car. Driving a car is a privilege, not a right, and provides an opportunity for your son to demonstrate responsible behavior. The decision to allow this privilege can be evaluated on the basis of how he maintains the car, checks in with you to let you know where he is, and follows his curfew. Driving a car is a powerful motivator for a teenager to do the right thing.

Limit your son's exposure to and experience with crime and violence. If guns or other weapons are kept in or around the house, they must be locked away and completely inaccessible to unsupervised children and adolescents.

8. Give them safe opportunities to earn your trust.

Create safe places for teenage boys to congregate, in or outside the home. Accept their interests, and show that you're curious about them. Boys are much more likely to talk while engaged in an activity. Praise them when it works. Positive experiences will build their self-esteem and self-reliance and help keep them connected.

Find ways for your son to gain experience doing socially necessary and responsible work.

Honor his need for personal space. Often he may need the time to digest disappointing or sad experiences. He likely will be ready to talk about it at a later, possibly unexpected time. For example, he may be ready to talk at 10 p.m. on the way home from a hockey game. He'll be strapped in a seat belt, so you know he can't get away!

Ask your son his opinions about issues, ideas, family matters, current events, and television programs. These conversations will demonstrate your respect for his ideas and give him the chance to think through and articulate his own thoughts. Validate him as a thinking person and show that you care about his opinions.

Barney Brawer, a former school principal, suggests: "I might recommend to a mother that sometimes, if you help your son fix his bike, at the end of an hour and a half of fiddling with the darned thing to get the gears smooth, you'll find yourself having the conversation with your son that earlier at dinner he was unwilling to have about his day or what courses he wanted to take."

— *Carey Goldberg, "Growing Move to Address a Cultural Threat to Boys"*

9. Try small conversations instead of extended discussions or lectures.

Address issues in small bites. Boys respond better to fewer questions than more. They may give less information than you want, but that's as much as they can give at one time.

Try to ask specific, pointed questions about their day. For example: "What did your coach work on in soccer practice? Did you discuss freedom of speech in your American history class?" If you ask general questions, such as "How was school?" you'll get evasive and uninformative answers, such as "Good."

Try to talk to them during or immediately after an activity. Boys seem to be more comfortable communicating in spontaneous conversations related to the moment. They are less comfortable with agendas. Stay connected through their interests. They build from these links as they get older.

Nothing stops a conversation with an adolescent boy more quickly than an interrogation. Subtle forms of communication are more likely to invoke a meaningful response.

Try not to lecture. How you present information will determine whether he allows himself to become engaged. Mothers need to speak and learn to understand a "boy's language." At the same time, mothers can subtly teach them the language of women. Mothers (and fathers) tend to give more information than boys want to hear. Remember, most people — adults and teenagers — can only take in a limited amount of information at one time.

10. Don't be disappointed when you believe you have an opportunity to talk, but your son is not ready, and, therefore, acts as if he's uninterested.

Don't misinterpret "not ready" as a desire to be disconnected.

Be available at other times, because you never know when that

ZITS   **BY JERRY SCOTT AND JIM BORGMAN**

Reprinted with special permission of King Features Syndicate.

teachable moment will occur. For example, older teenagers may want to talk when they get home on weekend nights. They're more relaxed then, even though you might prefer to be sleeping. Driving also provides a good opportunity to talk because you have a captive audience with few distractions. At the same time, try to understand their need for privacy. They'll communicate more freely if they don't feel you're being intrusive. Also respect their need to be silent, and don't be insulted or intimidated by it. Don't press when you know they've had enough.

Encourage communication by:
- approaching him in a safe, private place to minimize the possibility of embarrassment
- sharing your own feelings to normalize what he is feeling
- using brief statements
- giving him space
- touching on the feelings and then backing off, knowing you can come back to the subject later

11. Encourage involvement of fathers.

Fathers should help ensure that their sons stay close to their mothers.

Fathers should develop interests with their sons that they can do together. Like mothers, fathers should learn to appreciate non-verbal communication and to express love by doing activities together. Playing catch is a powerful connection.

Fathers need independent time with their sons. Often it's easier to connect as a twosome, and the time alone with your child can provide a special opportunity for communication. For adolescent boys, this smaller grouping carries less risk of embarrassment for him.

Even if boys feel more comfortable connecting emotionally with their mothers, boys should be encouraged to communicate with their fathers as well. Mothers can play a pivotal role in encouraging this to happen.

> I said to my son, "Well, have you told your father yet that you scratched the car?" Damon said, "No, do you want to tell him, Mom, or do you want me to tell him?" I answered, "Why don't you tell him?" Even though he still wanted me to be the mediator, I encouraged him to talk to his dad directly. I still do that with a lot of things rather than being the go-between. —*Focus Group Mother*

12. **Stay involved with your son's school from pre-school through high school.**

Get involved with school and community organizations and activities. Your involvement gives you an opportunity to see your son in a different setting, models what you value as important in the home, and, by getting to know teachers and coaches, helps to ensure that your child's needs are met when you're not present.

Talk to teachers about what you think your son needs to reinforce his success.

Promote inclusion of people of color in the curriculum, so that all children can gain an understanding of and appreciation for the contributions of diverse cultures to society.

Advocate for the ways in which your son learns best. He needs to be exposed to a variety of learning strategies to express what he knows, such as paper and pencil activities, hands-on activities, artistic expressions, and oral presentations.

Use surrogates, such as other adults with whom your son feels comfortable, as a resource. For example, when one of the mothers in a focus group became ill, she initiated regular discussions with a counselor at school who checked in with her son to make sure he was coping with his fears about her health. At home, he never expressed his emotions about his mother's illness, but he was able to work through his feelings with a competent and caring adult at school.

13. Love them for who they are!

Dr. Barbara Staggers shares: "With all the kids I know who make it, there's one thing in common: individual contact with an adult who cared and who kept hanging in there." —*Douglas Foster, "The Disease is Adolescence"*

Don't let one day go by without telling your son how much you love and appreciate him. Boys of all ages need physical affection and verbal expressions of love. Stay in touch. As they get older, it may appear that they need their parents less often. However, appearances can be deceiving: they still need you!

Try to see your son in action, whether it's at a sports game, a drama presentation, or a student art show. It's important to show him how much you value and support his interests and activities.

Use every opportunity, regardless of whether your son asks for it, to validate his increasingly hidden need to connect.

Finally, be alert and concerned, but maintain your sense of humor and perspective. Try to go with the flow as much as possible. While parents are a critical influence on their children, you can neither take all the blame nor all the responsibility for what children think and do.

The Power of Connection
How Can We Redefine Masculinity?

I n the context of respectfully fostering communication between the sexes, authors Shem and Surrey (1998) state, "Our goal is not to make men more like women... but to help both genders use their differences to create good connections with each other." Our hope is to communicate to you that boys have a "hidden yearning for relationship" (Pollack, 1998). However, most adolescent boys suffer from what Shem and Surrey (1998) call a "relational paradox" in which, for several years, their need for connection is in conflict with the cultural demand for them to become independent. When we look beyond this paradox, we find that boys have the capacity for empathy and benefit greatly from staying attached to their parents, close mentors, and positive peer friendships.

Shem and Surrey's research demonstrates that middle school student attitudes are a strong reflection of societal images. And despite the cultural pressure of gender roles and relationship stereotypes, boys are still in touch with a desire for connection. When 10- to 13-year-old girls were asked what strengths boys bring to relationships, they responded, "courage, muscle, strength, and laughter." Boys' responses to the same question about girls included "kindness, study buddies, and open about their feelings." However, when the question was changed to "What do you most want the other group to understand about you?" the answers were very different. Girls replied, "We aren't Barbie dolls. We are their equal, and when we're moody we're not always having PMS." Boys said, "Please see my heart. We're aggressive because we can't show our feelings any other way. We can be good friends with you" (Smith, 1998).

Yet our society communicates to parents, especially mothers, that attachments during certain times in a boy's life may rob a boy of his manhood. As Marianne Walters (1992) asks, "Do we have to throw the mother away with the apron?" When it comes to raising boys, many parents ignore their inner wisdom. Parents tend to be reactive rather than proactive, and allow society to dictate acceptable male behavior. We become more  concerned with protecting our boys from becoming "wimps" or acting feminine, because we understand that this shames them and may deprive them of their greatest male prize, power and privilege. So to protect our boys, we eliminate many creative, effective avenues of development. We celebrate only the traditional masculine avenues for affiliation, with sports being the most accessible and desirable.

Mental health experts are challenging the unquestioned obedience to the cultural and psychological straitjacket applied to boys. The dialogue has begun, and we can now analyze what we once automatically sanctioned as acceptable and non-acceptable behaviors, activities, and attitudes for boys. We don't agree with an emphasis on the need for "win or lose" situations; competition alone fails to give boys sufficient equipment in their emotional toolbox.

We also disagree with the men's movement as defined by Robert Bly (1990), which asserts that men feel lost and ineffectual because they're not properly initiated into manhood by their male elders and have lost touch with the "wild-man" in themselves. This "wild-man" theory focuses on the past, emphasizing collective human history and the need for men to develop their "inner warrior."

The answers to fulfilling the need for human connection don't lie buried in the deep past of human history. Rather, the challenge of raising fully developed and balanced young men is a contemporary problem that requires contemporary solutions. These solutions must include maintaining the hard-earned, expanded, acceptable options for women while expanding the possibilities for men.

The role of parents and other adults is larger than merely helping boys to navigate the tests of the physical world. Fathers don't have to bully or hit their sons to keep them in line or toughen them up. In fact, "simply by being close to their male offspring they have a pacifying effect on their behavior" (Prothrow-Stith and Weissmann, 1991). Beyond sports and occasional daredevil behavior, the more extreme physical tests include combat, gang activity, and violence. Consider the fact that 30,000 males are killed every year by firearms, more than the death toll during two years of the Vietnam War (Centers for Disease Control and Prevention, 1997). We should ask ourselves, is this a culture worth celebrating or is it putting boys in great jeopardy? Perhaps to heighten awareness of the danger, we should consider building a memorial to all of the boys who died worshiping the only culture they knew with the only skills they had.

Boys' discomfort with intimacy is "why boys don't talk"; this discomfort is the powerful downside of a boy's quest for power and privilege. Just as women are encouraged to be intimate and comfortable in relationships at the cost of giving up their ability to express anger or act assertively, boys are encouraged to be independent and powerful at the expense of losing intimacy skills. A man's fear of failure and discomfort with intimacy comes from his need to have others reaffirm his competence. For women, the lack of power often leads to the fear of success.

Given this dichotomy, it bears repeating that each gender is asked to halve itself (Silverstein and Rashbaum, 1994). We may be partially

Today, an African American boy in an urban area is more likely to die of a gunshot wound than was an African American male who served in the Vietnam war; of the millions of "boys" who went to Vietnam, 59,000 were killed. —*Michael Gurian, The Wonder of Boys*

biologically "hard-wired" or predisposed to recreate traditional roles, but we can still step in and create a supportive environment where each gender can work harder on the less developed part.

We believe that parents can make a difference in the lives of their children. If there is one message that you take away from this book, it is this: Mothers are not the enemy of their son's independence. We offer our sons the skills and tools to communicate and build connections that can result in a more satisfying life, for them and us. These skills will also provide our sons with the tools to express their dark side in ways that are more appropriate and less potentially harmful to themselves and to others.

Parents can offset the culture of violence in which boys are immersed. According to Robert Sampson and John Laub (1994), among the 500 boys they studied recently, they found that the parent/child relationship is almost always the controlling factor as to whether the child would or would not become a delinquent. Laub says that three parts of that relationship are especially significant: "intimacy in the younger years, consistent discipline, and careful parental supervision."

As parents, we must reverse what is becoming a dangerous tide of alienation and violence. But we don't have to do this alone. There are resources to support our efforts in raising our sons. The rewards of looking at these adolescent issues through a new lens include getting to know our sons better and enjoying them more. We want to end by reframing the old adage:

> **"A son is a son until he takes a wife,**
> **A daughter is a daughter for the rest of her life."**
> **to:**
> **"A son is a son though he may take a wife,**
> **and remains a son for the rest of his life."**

Positive Parenting — The Law of Return

"One good parent is worth 1000 schoolmasters."
—Chinese Proverb

The purpose of this parent brief is to present 14 principles of positive parenting:

1. Parenting is a process. You never arrive with all the skills that you need.
2. Parents are not trained to be parents; kids are not trained to be kids. Kids train parents; parents train kids.
3. It is more challenging to be a parent than to function in your job.
4. Parenting is a journey, not a destination.
5. Parents are the most significant influence in a child's life.
6. A parent is the greatest teacher a child will ever have. A parent and child certainly have the longest teaching relationship ever known.
7. It is not a question of whether a parent is a teacher or not, it's a question of what is taught. Parents teach kids a whole language before they come to school.
8. If you pay attention to your child, he will teach you what you need to learn.
9. Parent modeling that includes the unspoken as well as the spoken word is the most powerful force in shaping a child's life.
10. How you spend your time and money tells your kids what you value, regardless of what you say.
11. Successful parenting is predictable, reliable, and consistent.
12. There's no greater investment in life than children.
13. Parents that praise each of their children at least twice a day maintain a positive relationship regardless of the problems they encounter.
14. Behind every successful child is a loving parent.

Developed by The Mid-Atlantic Equity Center. Chevy Chase, MD: 1998.

Overview of Focus Groups

What are focus groups?

A focus group is a carefully planned discussion designed to obtain a selected group of individuals' perceptions regarding a defined area of interest.

Key Characteristics of a Focus Group

- **Focus Groups Involve People**

  Focus groups are typically composed of six to twelve people — large enough for everyone to exchange ideas and options, but small enough for everyone to participate in the discussion. Participants are selected based on common demographic characteristics or experiences. They share something that directly relates to the topic being studied, and are usually somewhat familiar with the topic.

- **Focus Groups Are Conducted In Series**

  Multiple focus groups are held to draw out patterns. This is important because multiple sessions increase the reliability of the results. The more complex the issue, the more focus groups you need to schedule. However, after a certain point, additional sessions become redundant and add little unique information.

- **Focus Groups Are A Data Collection Procedure**

  Focus groups are held to learn about why and how a particular group of people approach an issue. They are frequently used to evaluate a program or policy or to understand product marketing.

  Focus groups yield information about the perspective of a target group — how it perceives, feels, and thinks about a specific product, service, or opportunity. They are not intended to reach consensus or decide on potential courses of action.

- **Focus Groups Have A Focused Discussion**

  Focus groups are led by a moderator who seeks to create a non-threatening environment for all participants. The topics are predetermined and organized prior to the session. The moderator uses a detailed discussion guide of open-ended questions that follow a logical sequence. This discussion guide addresses topics and specific questions relating to the purpose of the focus group. In general, participants have little input into its content. Discussion typically runs from ninety minutes to two and one half hours. Responses and observations are recorded on the spot.

Advantages of Focus Groups
- Increase "face validity" (apparent validity) because the data collection process places a premium on individual contributions.
- Provide an economical data collection option, depending on the number of groups conducted and locations selected.
- Capture a wider range of responses than individual interviews.
- Reveal insights and nuances that other research methods, such as surveys, usually cannot.

The decision whether to use focus groups depends on:
- The purpose of the study.
- The questions being asked.
- The type of data needed.
- Resource availability (time and cost).

Use focus groups:
- To understand how people feel and think about a program, service, or issue.
- To test an exploratory design as a preliminary study.

Qualitative and Quantitative Research Methods
Focus groups are a tool often used in "qualitative" research, research that does not use statistical methods as the primary means to gather and sort information. Instead of the numbers used in quantitative research, qualitative research is marked by observation — words which describe the issue in question.

Ideally, you will be able to use both quantitative and qualitative methods to learn more about the topic in which you are interested. Neither method is inherently superior. Quantitative and qualitative methods complement each other and are each suited to answer different types of questions.

Elements	Qualitative	Quantitative
Purpose	To describe a situation, gain insight into a particular practice, belief, etc.	To predict something to reveal the prevalence — how widespread is something?
Format	No predetermined response categories (e.g., question could ask "How satisfied are you with XYZ program?")	Standardized measures, response categories pre-determined and pre-supplied (e.g., responses could range from "not at all satisfied" to "completely satisfied")
Resulting Data	In-depth explanatory data from a small, representative segment of the population	Breadth of data from a large statistically representative segment of the population
Limitation	Complicates the issues, cannot generalize results to larger population	Simplifies the issue, can generalize results to larger population
Framework	Draws out pattern from concepts and insights	Tests a hypothesis, uses data to support a conclusion; may use a control group
Process	Illustrative explanation and individual responses	Numerical aggregation in the form of percentages, tables, etc.; responses are clustered
Approach	Subjective	Objective
Analysis	Interpretative — how and why	Statistical — what and how many
Analytical Strength	"Face" validity — the results usually look valid	Statistical reliability
Methods	Varied format for group and individual interviews: direct observation	Standardized interviews, surveys, regression analysis

Adapted from Simply Better, Continuous Improvement, Customers In Focus: A Guide to Conducting and Planning Focus Groups, Project Coordinator, Frank Wilson, pp. 1–6.
Developed by Dr. Joyce Kaser and Susan Rosshirt, 1999.

Focus Group Interview Guide — Adolescents

1. Are you glad that you are a girl/boy? Why? Can you identify particular traits about girls/boys that you are happy to have?

2. Do people treat you differently because you are a girl/boy? Teachers? Parents? If you have a sibling of the opposite gender, is there a difference in how your parents treat him or her? Peers of the opposite sex? Strangers? Coaches? Other members of your own sex?

3. Do people treat you differently because of your race, culture, or ethnicity? If so, how does it make you feel? How do you respond?

4. How would you describe your friends? How are they like or unlike you? How do you choose your friends? Do they have to be cool? What do you describe as cool? What sort of things do you and your friends do together (music, sports, talk, hang out)?

5. Do you have close friends of the opposite sex? What is it about these friends that you like? What do you see as the difference between a close friend of the opposite sex and a boyfriend or girlfriend? How are your close same-sex friends different from your close friends of the opposite sex?

6. What sort of group activities do you participate in (in or out of school)? Sports, bands, clubs? How do you decide which groups to join?

7. Describe your relationships with adults in your lives. Are they good or bad? Parents and other adult family members, teachers, counselors, coaches?

8. If your relationships with the adults you have just described are bad, what do you think could be done to make them good?

9. Do you ever feel angry? What/who makes you angry? What do you do with your anger? What is the worst name you could be called?

10. Do you ever feel sad? What/who makes you sad? What do you do with your sadness?

11. When you have a problem, what do you do? Do you seek advice from others? Who?

12. What are your feelings about homosexuality? Do you know any homosexual students? Do you or others treat them differently from your other friends?

13. What can you do to change the way people treat your gender and think about your gender? How can you work with others for change?

Focus Group Interview Guide — Parents

1. What qualities do you look for in your son?
2. Are there specific masculine traits?
3. What are the challenges of raising your son in a culture different from your own?
4. Have you noticed a time when your relationship with your son changed? If so, when did this occur?
5. Do you treat him differently as a result of this change?
6. How does he treat you?
7. If you also have a daughter, do you treat her differently than your son? If so, how?
8. How do you view displays of anger and sadness?
9. How does your son deal with anger and sadness?
10. How do you deal with conflict with your son?
11. Do you know who your son's friends are?
12. Does your son experience pressure to hang out with one group over another?
13. What kind of experiences in school has your son had?
14. What kind of interests does your son have?
15. Does your son talk on the phone? With whom?
16. What are some successful ways you can talk to him?
17. How would you describe the media presentation of boys?
18. Do you have any conflict with your spouse in terms of raising your son?
19. What are your hopes/fears for your son?

American Academy of Child and Adolescent Psychology's Stages of Normal Adolescent Development

Each teenager is an individual with a unique personality and special interests, likes, and dislikes. In general, however, there is a series of developmental tasks that everyone faces during the adolescent years.

A teenager's development can be divided into three stages — early, middle, and late adolescence. The normal feelings and behaviors of adolescents for each stage are described below.

Early Adolescence (12–14 years)
Movement Towards Independence
Struggle with sense of identity
Moodiness
Improved abilities to use speech to express oneself
More likely to express feelings by action than by words
Close friendships gain importance
Less attention shown to parents, with occasional rudeness
Realization that parents are not perfect; identification of their faults
Search for new people to love in addition to parents
Tendency to return to childish behavior, fought off by excessive activity
Peer group influence on interests and clothing styles

Career Interests
Mostly interested in present and near future
Greater ability to work

Sexuality
Girls ahead of boys
Same-sex friends and group activities
Shyness, blushing, and modesty
Show-off qualities
Greater interest in privacy
Experimentation with body (masturbation)
Worries about being normal

Ethics and Self-Direction
Rule and limit testing
Occasional experimentation with cigarettes, marijuana, and alcohol
Capacity for abstract thought

Middle Adolescence (15–16 Years)
Movement Towards Independence
Self-involvement, alternating between unrealistically high expectations and poor self-concept
Complaints that parents interfere with independence
Extremely concerned with appearance and with one's own body
Feelings of strangeness about one's self and body
Lowered opinion of parents, withdrawal of emotions from them
Effort to make new friends
Strong emphasis on the new peer group with the group identity of selectivity, superiority, and competitiveness
Periods of sadness as the psychological loss of the parents takes place
Examination of inner experiences, which may include writing a diary

Career Interests
Intellectual interests gain importance
Some sexual and aggressive energies directed into creative and career interests

Sexuality
Concerns about sexual attractiveness
Frequently changing relationships
Movement towards heterosexuality with fears of homosexuality
Tenderness and fears shown towards opposite sex
Feelings of love and passion

Ethics and Self-Description
Development of ideals and selection of role models
More consistent evidence of conscience
Greater capacity for setting goals
Interest in moral reasoning

Late Adolescence (17–19 years)
Movement Towards Independence
Firmer identity

Ability to delay gratification

Ability to think ideas through

Ability to express ideas in words

More developed sense of humor

Stable interests

Greater emotional stability

Ability to make independent decisions

Ability to compromise

Pride in one's work

Self-reliance

Greater concern for others

Career Interests
More defined work habits

Higher level of concern for the future

Thoughts about one's role in life

Sexuality
Concerned with serious relationships

Clear sexual identity

Capacities for tender and sensual love

Ethics and Self-Direction
Capable of useful insight

Stress on personal dignity and self-esteem

Ability to set goals and follow through

Acceptance of social institutions and cultural traditions

Self-regulation of self esteem

Teenagers will naturally vary slightly from the descriptions in the charts above, but the feelings and behaviors listed for each area are, in general, considered normal for each of the three stages. The mental and emotional problems that can interfere with these normal developmental stages are treatable.

If a teenager seems very different from the descriptions presented here, it may be appropriate to consult with a mental health professional.

1996 Center for Adolescent Studies - Indiana University.
<www.education.indiana.edu/cas/adol/development.html>

Listening to Boys' Voices:
Results of 1998 McLean Hospital Survey of Boys' Self-Esteem and Definitions of Masculinity

A recent study, titled "Listening to Boys' Voices," involved over 200 boys between the ages of 12 and 18 (grades 7–12) who lived in the Northeastern United States. Subjects came from primarily middle class, Caucasian families. Ten percent were African American, Hispanic, or Asian American. Designed to measure self-esteem, attitudes about gender roles, depression and sadness, unconscious attitudes and feelings about self and others as well as egalitarian attitudes toward boys and girls, the study involved empirical testing, one-on-one interviews, and psychological inventories specifically designed to measure subconscious emotional states.

Study findings indicate:

- Boys are confronting a double standard of masculinity. Boys score high on scales of gender role equality or egalitarianism (e.g., "Men and women deserve equal pay," "Boys and girls should both be allowed to express feelings," "There is no such thing as 'men's work or women's work,'" etc.) but at the same time continue to endorse traditional male role beliefs (e.g., "It is essential for a guy to get respect," and "Men are always ready for sex.")

- As boys mature, they feel increased pressure to conform to an aggressive dominant male stereotype which leads to low self-esteem and high incidence of depression. For example, when asked if "guys must be sure of themselves," 81 percent of young boys (grades 7–9) said yes while almost 100 percent of older boys (grades 10–12) agreed. When asked if boys must "be ready for sex," 66 percent of young boys said yes while 76 percent of older boys said yes. The study shows a significant correlation between those who agreed with traditional masculine propositions about sex and an increased incidence of depression.

- As boys grow older, they feel greater pressure to mask feelings of low self-esteem. Although the boys in the study had normal range self-esteem scores, the number of false responses was dramatically high and increased with age.

- Boys feel significant anxiety and sadness about growing up to be men. They view manhood as filled with unrewarding work, isolation from friends and family, and unhappiness and disappointment.

- Despite appearing outwardly content, many boys feel deep feelings of loneliness and alienation.

- Social withdrawal followed by outreach for emotional connection. Almost 90 percent of boys said they felt the need to withdraw initially when they felt strong feelings of sadness or vulnerability. Boys initially will withdraw as a way to handle vulnerability, but then will re-emerge. Understanding this pattern of emotional behavior is a breakthrough in helping to explain the emotional and psychological needs of boys as well as identifying the moment for reconnection.

- Heightened sensitivity to shame. Over 50 percent of boys spoke of "daily shame" and taunts about masculinity, courage, and integrity.

- Boys find heroes/role models within family. When asked who boys considered to be their most important role models, mentors, and heroes, over 75 percent of boys identified a parent, grandparent, or sibling.

"Boys today are struggling under a double standard about what it means to become the 'new man' versus the 'traditional guy,'" reports William Pollack, Ph.D. "This inner confusion is reflected in boys' conflicting ideas about gender roles, an increase in feelings of sadness and incidence of depression, and lying to cover concerns about self-esteem. The initial phases of this study show that this double standard causes a great deal of angst and resistance for boys as they mature in contemporary society. The time has come to change the way boys are raised — in our homes, in our schools, and in society."

Adapted from "Adolescence is Time of Crisis for Even 'Healthy' Boys, Finds McLean Study." Boston, MA: McLean Hospital Press Release, June 4, 1998.

How Vulnerable Is My Teen to Depression?

How can you identify the root causes of a child's depression and steer him toward help? Since much of adolescent depression is a reaction to a combination of stress factors, you can begin by considering the following questions. Be alert to the fact that several yes answers in combination over the past year can indicate that your child is especially vulnerable to depression.

1. Has your child experienced the loss of an important family member or friend during the last year?

2. Have you and your spouse had significant marital problems resulting in prolonged conflict or tension?

3. Are you and your child's other parent divorced? If so, is your child often asked to relay messages from one parent to the other? Have you communicated to your son that he's now the man of the house?

4. Has your child switched schools with little or no access to his old friends?

5. Does your teenager have a chronic illness which limits his activity and/or isolates him?

6. Do you have high expectations of your child and find yourself disappointed — allowing your child to know that he failed to reach your expectations?

7. Is someone in your family very critical of your son? Is he often referred to as the "difficult one"?

8. Are you a strict or rigid parent with a low tolerance for conflict or disagreements?

9. Are you overly permissive with very few rules and regulations?

10. Do you communicate either verbally or non-verbally that expressing anger is not tolerated in your home?

11. Does your teenager seem to often be the target of criticism, teasing, or indifference from peers?

12. Does your teenager have difficulty making and maintaining friendships?

Be aware that boys act out depression through many behaviors, some of which look different from classical depression. Even if your son isn't especially vulnerable to depression based on the above questions, pay close attention to any symptoms of depression you may notice, including:

- Fatigue

- Losing joy in activities he previously enjoyed

- Increased intensity

- Increased aggression

- New interest in "self medication" (alcohol or drugs)

- Shift in interest level in sexual encounters

- Harsh self-criticism

- Difficulty concentrating

- Denial of pain

- Over involvement with academic work or sports

American Academy of Child and Adolescent Psychiatry
1999 Violence Fact Sheet

- In 1996, the National Center on Child Abuse and Neglect reported 969,018 cases of violent crimes committed against children.

- In 1996–97, ten percent of all public schools reported at least one serious violent crime to police or law enforcement (Bureau of Justice Statistics and Office of Juvenile Justice and Delinquency Prevention, U.S. Department of Justice).

- Gunshot wounds to children ages 16 and under have increased 300 percent in major urban areas since 1986.

- According to FBI reports, 2,900 juveniles were arrested for murder in 1996.

- Estimates indicate that as many as 5,000 children die each year as a result of mistreatment and abuse from parents or guardians.

- Everyday in America 16 children and youths are killed by firearms (Children's Defense Fund, 1998).

- Nearly a million U.S. students took guns to school during 1998 (Parents Resource Institute for Drug Education).

- Each year 123,400 children are arrested for violent crimes in the U.S. (Office of Juvenile Justice and Juvenile Delinquency Prevention, 1997).

- Persons under age 25 make up nearly 50 percent of all victims of a serious violent crime (The Institute for Youth Development, 1998).

The American Academy of Child and Adolescent Psychiatry.
<www.aacap.org/info_families/NationalFacts/99ViolFctSh.htm>, 1999.

Guns, Gangs, Harmful Threats, and Injury Are Part of Teen Lives:

The 1997-98 National Parents' Resource Institute for Drug Education (PRIDE) Survey of Grades 6-12

While at school have you...	%
Carried a gun?	3.8
Carried a knife, club, or other weapon?	16.9
Threatened a student with a gun, knife, or club?	6.1
Threatened to hurt a student by hitting, slapping, or kicking?	39.9
Hurt a student by using a gun, knife, or club?	4.0
Hurt a student by hitting, slapping, or kicking?	30.9
Been threatened with a gun, knife, or club by a student?	10.4
Had a student threaten to hit, slap, or kick you?	39.4
Been afraid a student may hurt you?	23.5
Been hurt by a student using a gun, knife, or club?	3.0
Been hurt by a student who hit, slapped, or kicked you?	17.6

While NOT at school have you...	
Carried a gun?	15.6
Carried a knife, club, or other weapon?	29.9
Been threatened with a gun, knife, or club by a student?	10.2
Been threatened by a student to beat you up?	28.7
Been hurt by a student using a gun, knife, or club?	4.0

Other questions	
Do you take part in gang activities?	10.8
Have you thought about committing suicide?	29.2
Have you been in trouble with the police?	24.3
Do your parents set clear rules for you? (Often/A Lot)	67.7
Do your parents punish you when you break the rules? (Often/A Lot)	53.3

PRIDE Surveys News Release. November 1, 1999 ‹www.prideusa.org›.

What Can You Do if You Suspect Your Child Is Involved in a Gang?

1. Don't ignore your suspicions; talk to your child.

2. Watch for signs of involvement, including the use of unexplained symbols in tattoos, jewelry, and other personal possessions, money from an unexplained source, new friends that your child will not allow you to meet, and frequent negative contacts with the police.

3. Listen to conversations your child has with friends or new acquaintances.

4. Check your child's room periodically for signs or symbols.

5. Talk to your child's teachers about your suspicions.

6. Divert your child's attention away from friends unknown to you and into other activities.

7. Ask for help from the many community agencies.

8. Call the police. They will respond to your questions and if desired talk with you and your child about gangs.

Do not think that a gang is just a phase. Older gang members use newer gang members or people looking to get into the gang by having them take most of the risk. Large quantities of cocaine have been found on newer members, while older members refuse to associate with them when they get caught.

Dane County Narcotics and Gang Task Force. Madison, WI: 1999. <www.ci.madison.wi.us/police/gangfaqs.html>.

References

Adams, B. "Change and Continuity in the U.S. Family Today." *Bangladesh Journal of Sociology,* 1998.

Albom, M. *Tuesdays with Morrie.* New York: Doubleday, 1997.

American Academy of Child and Adolescent Psychiatry. *1999 Violence Fact Sheet.* Washington, DC: AACAP, 1999.

American Academy of Child and Adolescent Psychology. *Stages of Normal Adolescent Development.* December 4, 1999 <www.education.indiana.edu/cas/adol/development.html>.

American Association of University Women. Hostile Hallways: *The AAUW Survey on Sexual Harassment in America's Schools.* Washington, DC: AAUW, 1993.

————.*Separated by Sex: A Critical Look at Single-Sex Education for Girls.* Washington, DC: AAUW, 1998.

American Youth Policy Forum. *The Forgotten Half Revisited.* Washington, DC: AYPF, 1998.

Anderson, R., K. Kochanek, and S. Murphy. *Report of Final Mortality Statistics.* Washington, DC: Centers for Disease Control and Prevention, 1995.

Barnard, L. "For Crying Out Loud." *The Toronto Sun,* February 23, 1998 <www.thepaperboy.com>.

Begley, S. "Gray Matters." *Newsweek,* March 27, 1995:48-54.

Belitz, J., and D. Valdez. "Clinical Issues in the Treatment of Chicano Male Gang Youths." A. Padilla, Ed. *Hispanic Psychology: Critical Issues in Theory and Research* (148-165). Thousand Oaks, CA: Sage Publications, 1995.

Belkin, L. "Getting the Girl." *The New York Times Magazine,* July 25, 1999:26-31, 38, 54-55.

————. "Parents Blaming Parents." *The New York Times Magazine,* October 31, 1999:94, 100.

Belluck, P. "Reason Is Sought for Lag by Blacks in School Effort." *The New York Times,* July 4, 1999:1,12.

Bening, A. Interview on "The Today Show." *NBC,* October 1999.

Betcher, W. *A Time of Fallen Heroes: The Re-Creation of Masculinity.* New York: Guilford Press, 1995.

Bly, R. *Iron John: A Book about Men.* Reading, MA: Addison-Wesley, 1990.

Bodinger-deUriarte, C. *Membership in Violent Gangs Fed by Suspicion, Deterred through Respect.* Los Alamitos, CA: Southwest Regional Educational Laboratory, 1993.

Bordo, S. *The Male Body: A New Look at Men in Public and in Private.* New York: Farrar, Straus & Giroux, 1999.

Bowlby, B. *Attachment and Loss.* New York: Basic Books, 1980.

Brady, E. "Cancer Gave Torre New Outlook on the Game." *USA Today,* October 28, 1999:C1, 2.

Britt, D. "Tough Lessons Behind the Wheel." *The Washington Post,* July 17, 1998:C1.

Buddha Monk. "Land of My Dreams." *The Prophecy.* New York: Edel America Records, 1999.

Burnett, G., and G. Walz. "Gangs in the Schools." *ERIC Digest 99,* July 1994.

Bushweller, K. "Turning Our Back on Boys." *The American School Board Journal,* May 1994:20-25.

Casas, J., et al. "Hispanic Masculinity: Myth or Psychological Schema Meriting Clinical Consideration." A. Padilla, Ed. *Hispanic Psychology: Critical Issues in Theory and Research* (231-244). Thousand Oaks, CA: Sage Publications, 1995.

Centers for Disease Control and Prevention. *Monthly Vital Statistics Report,* 45(11)S2:57, 1997.

Children Now. "Boys to Men: Entertainment Media - Messages about Masculinity." November 10, 1999 <www.childrennow.org>.

Children's Defense Fund. "Frequently Asked Questions." *The State of America's Children Yearbook.* Washington, DC: CDF, 1997.

Cleage, P. *What Looks Like Crazy on an Ordinary Day.* New York: Avon Books, 1992.

Clines, F. "The Therapy Question." *The New York Times,* September 17, 1998 <www.nytimes.com>.

Cohn, D. "Single Father Households on the Rise." *The Washington Post,* December 11, 1998:A1, 6-7.

Comer, J., and A. Poussaint. *Raising Black Children.* New York: Plume, 1992.

Coontz, S. *The Way We Really Are: Coming to Terms with America's Changing Families.* New York: Harper Collins, 1997.

Cooper, C., J. Denner, and E. Lopez. "Cultural Brokers: Helping Latino Children on Toward Success." *The Future of Children When School is Out,* 9(2):51-56, Fall 1999.

Dane County Narcotics and Gang Task Force. *What Can You Do if You Suspect Your Child Is Involved in a Gang?* October 15, 1999, <www.ci.madison.wi.us/police/gangfaqs.html>.

Derman-Sparks, L., and A.B.C. Task Force. *Anti-Bias Curriculum: Tools for Empowering Young Children.* Washington, DC: National Association for the Education of Young Children, 1989.

Donahue, P. L., et al. *NAEP 1998 Reading Report Card for the Nation and the States.* Washington, DC: U.S. Department of Education, 1999.

Edelman, M.W. *Guide My Feet: Prayers and Meditations on Loving and Working for Children.* New York: Harper Perennial Library, 1996.

Egan, T. "From Adolescent Angst to Shooting Up Schools." *The New York Times,* June 14, 1998:1.

Engber, A., and L. Klungness. *The Complete Single Mother.* Holbrook, MA: Adams Media Corporation, 1995.

Erikson, E. *Childhood and Society.* New York: W. W. Norton, 1963.

———. *Identity, Youth, and Crisis.* New York: W. W. Norton, 1994.

Faludi, S. "The Betrayal of the American Man." *Newsweek,* September 13, 1999: 48-58.

Federal Interagency Forum on Child and Family Statistics. *America's Children: Key National Indicators of Well-Being.* Washington, DC: U.S. Government Printing Office, 1999.

Fivush, R. "Exploring Sex Differences in the Emotional Content of Mother-Child Conversation About the Past." *Sex Role,* 20(11/12):675-691, 1989.

Ford, D. *Reversing Underachievement among Gifted Black Students: Promising Practices and Programs.* New York: Teachers College (Columbia University), 1996.

Fordham, S., and J. Ogbu. "Black Students' School Success: Coping with the Burden of 'Acting White.'" *Urban Review,* 18:176-206, 1986.

Foster, D. "The Disease Is Adolescence." *Rolling Stone,* December 9, 1993:55-60, 78.

Friedan, B. *The Feminine Mystique.* New York: W. W. Norton and Co., 1997.

Garbarino, J. *Lost Boys: Why Our Sons Turn Violent and How We Can Save Them.* New York: Free Press, 1999.

Gilligan, J. "Boys to Men: Questions of Violence." *Harvard Education Letter Research Online* (Forum Feature July/August 1999), August 10, 1999 <www.edletter.org/forum>

———. *Violence: Reflections on a National Epidemic.* New York: Vintage Books, 1997.

Goldberg, C. "Growing Move to Address a Cultural Threat to Boys." *The New York Times on the Web,* April 23, 1998 <www.nytimes.com/yr/mo/day/news/national/boys-studies>.

Gottman, J., and J. DeClaire. *The Heart of Parenting: Raising an Emotionally Intelligent Child.* New York: Simon & Schuster, 1997.

Greenfield, P., and J. Juvonen. "A Developmental Look at Columbine." *APA Monitor,* July/August 1999:33.

Gurian, M. *A Fine Young Man.* New York: Putnam, 1998.

———. *The Wonder of Boys.* New York: Tarcher/Putnam, 1996.

Gutkind, L. *Stuck in Time.* New York: Henry Holt and Company, 1993.

Hall, Stephen. "The Bully in the Mirror." *The New York Times Magazine,* August 22, 1999:31-35, 58, 62-65.

Hardiman, R., B. Jackson, and J. Kim. *Growing Up Racially.* Amherst, MA: New Perspective Inc., 1986.

Harris, J. R. *The Nurture Assumption.* New York: The Free Press, 1998.

Henderson, N. "What Makes School Good for Boys." *The Washington Post,* January 8, 1999:6-8.

Hornblower, M. "Beyond the Gender Myths." *Time,* October 19, 1998:90-91.

Hughes, L., A. Rampersad, and D. Roessel, Eds. "Mother and Son." *The Collected Poems of Langston Hughes.* New York: Knopf, 1994.

Jackson, L. *Gangbusters: Strategies for Prevention and Intervention.* Upper Marlboro, MD: Graphic Communications, Inc., 1998.

Jones, R. "I Don't Feel Safe Here Anymore: Your Legal Duty to Protect Gay Kids from Harassment." *The American School Board Journal,* November 1999: 26-31.

Kantrowitz, B., and C. Kalb. "Boys Will Be Boys." *Newsweek,* May 11, 1998: 54-60.

Kaser, J., and S. Rosshirt. *Overview of Focus Groups.* Developed as a Resource for Researchers, 1999.

Katz, J. *Tough Guise: Violence, Media and the Crisis in Masculinity.* Northampton, MA: Media Education Foundation, 1999.

Katz, J., and S. Jhally. "The National Conversation in the Wake of Littleton Is Missing the Mark." *Boston Globe,* May 2, 1999:E1.

Kavanaugh, J. "I Knew This Kid." *Will You Be My Friend?* Kalamazoo, MI: Steven J. Nash, 1991.

Kenworthy, T. "'Help Us Heal,' Clinton Urges Columbine." *The Washington Post,* May 21, 1999:A15.

Kim, H. *Diversity among Asian American High School Students.* Princeton Educational Testing Service <www.ets.org>, 1997.

Kimmel, M. "What Are Little Boys Made Of?" *US,* October/November 1999: 88-91.

Kivel, P. *Boys Will Be Men: Raising Our Sons for Courage, Caring, and Community* Gabriola Island, BC, Canada: New Society Publishers, 1999.

LeBlanc, A. N. "The Outsiders." *The New York Times Magazine,* August 22, 1999:36-41.

Levant, R. F. *Masculinity Reconstructed: Changing the Rules of Manhood - At Work, in Relationships, and in Family Life.* New York: Dutton, 1995.

Levy, S. "Loitering on the Dark Side." *Newsweek,* May 3,1999:39.

Lichter, S., et al. *Prime Time: How TV Portrays American Culture.* Washington, DC: Regney Publications, 1994.

Majors, R., and J. Billson. Cool Pose: *The Dilemmas of Black Manhood in America.* New York: Lexington Books, 1992.

Marin, R. "At-Home Fathers Step Out to Find They Are Not Alone." *The New York Times,* January 2, 2000:1.

Maryland State Department of Education. *Maryland State Parents and Pupils* <www.msde.state.md.us>, 1997.

McLean Hospital Center for Men. *Adolescence Is Time of Crisis for Even "Healthy" Boys, Finds McLean Study.* Boston, MA: Mclean Hospital Press Release, June 4, 1998.

Mead, M. *Male and Female: The Classic Study of the Sexes.* New York: Quill, 1996.

Media Action Network for Asian Americans (MANAA). "Asian Stereotypes: Restrictive Portrayals of Asians in the Media and How to Balance Them." November 29, 1999 <www.janet.org/~manaa>.

Meltz, B. "Boys Need Moms Too." *Boston Globe,* November 7, 1998 <www.boston.com/dailyglobe>.

Messner, M. "Boyhood, Organized Sports, and the Construction of Masculinities." *Journal of Contemporary Ethnography,* 18(4):416-444, 1990.

Miller, J., and I. Stiver. *Healing Connection: How Women Form Relationships in Therapy and in Life.* Boston: Beacon Press, 1997.

Montgomery County Youth Workers Training Committee. "Young and Male: How to Nurture Adolescent Boys into Loving and Responsible Men." Educators' Training Workshop, November 20, 1998.

Murray, B. "Boys to Men: Emotional Miseducation." *APA Monitor,* 30(7):1, 38 39, July/August 1999.

National Center for Education Statistics. *National Assessment of Educational Progress (NAEP),* Writing Assessment. Washington, DC: 1998.

National Institute on Drug Abuse. "High School and Youth Trends." *Monitoring the Future Study,* 1996.

National Institute of Mental Health. "Suicide Facts, 1996." December 12, 1999 <www.nimh.gov/research/suifact.htm>.

National Parents' Resource Institute for Drug Education. "Guns, Gangs, Harmful Threats, and Injury Are Part of Teen Lives: the 1997-98 PRIDE Survey of Grades 6-12." *PRIDE Surveys News Release.* November 1, 1999 <www.prideusa.org>.

National Research Council. *Improving Schooling for Language- Minority Students: A Research Agenda.* Washington, DC: National Academy Press, 1997.

National Urban League. *The State of Black America 1998.* New York: National Urban League, 1998.

Niehoff, D. *The Biology of Violence.* New York: The Free Press, 1999.

Nightline with Ted Koppel. "The Sexuality Debate." November 23, 1999 <www.abcnews.go.com/onair/nightline>.

Noonan, P. "The Culture of Death." *The Wall Street Journal,* April 22, 1999:A22.

Norman, M. "From Carol Gilligan's Chair." *The New York Times Magazine,* November 9, 1997:50.

Oakes, J., et al. "Equity Lessons from Detracking Schools." 1997 ASCD Yearbook, *Rethinking Educational Change with Heart and Mind.* Alexandria, VA: Association for Supervision and Curriculum Development (ASCD), 1997.

O'Connor, J. "Letter to the Editor," *The New York Times Magazine,* September 12, 1999:18.

Ornish, D. *Love and Survival.* New York: Harper-Collins, 1997.

Osborne, J. "Race and Academic Disidentification." *Journal of Educational Psychology,* 89(4):728-35, December 1997.

Palladino, G. *Teenagers: An American History.* New York: Harper Collins, 1996.

Parke, R., and A. Brott. *Throwaway Dads.* Boston: Houghton Mifflin and Co., 1999.

Phillips, L. *The Girls Report: What We Know and Need to Know about Growing Up Female.* New York: The National Council for Research on Women, 1998.

Pollack, W. Real Boys: *Rescuing our Sons from the Myths of Boyhood.* New York: Random House, 1998.

Prince Georges County Public Schools. "What About Our Boys?" *Equity in our Schools,* 4(1):3-4, Fall 1999.

Prothrow-Stith, D., and M. Weissmann. *Deadly Consequences: How Violence Is Destroying Our Teenage Population and a Plan to Begin Solving the Problem.* New York: Harper Collins, 1991.

Real, T. *I Don't Want to Talk about It: Overcoming the Secret Legacy of Male Depression.* New York: Simon and Schuster, 1997.

Reilly, R. "The Good Father." *Sports Illustrated,* September 7, 1998:32-45.

Riordan, C. "The Silent Gender Gap: Reading, Writing, and Other Problems for Boys." *Education Week,* November 17, 1999:46, 49.

Rosenfeld, M. "Little Boys Blue: Reexamining the Plight of Young Males." *The Washington Post,* March 26, 1998:A1.

Ryan, J. "Boys to Men." *The San Francisco Chronicle,* March 22, 1998:1.

Sadker, M., and D. Sadker. *Failing at Fairness: How America's Schools Cheat Girls.* New York: Scribners, 1994.

Sampson, R., and J. Laub. "Urban Poverty and the Family Context of Delinquency: A New Look at Structure and Process in a Classic Study." *Child Development,* 65(2):523-40, April 1994.

Segal, L. *Slow Motion: Changing Masculinities, Changing Men.* New Jersey: Rutgers University Press, 1990.

Shaffer, S., and L. Shevitz. "She Bakes and He Builds: Gender Bias in the Curriculum." *Double Jeopardy: Addressing Gender Bias in Special Education Services.* New York: State University of New York Press, 1999.

Shapiro, L. "Guns and Dolls." *Newsweek,* May 28, 1998:56-65.

Shem, S., and J. Surrey. *We Have to Talk: Healing Dialogues Between Women and Men.* New York: Basic Books, 1998.

Siegler, A. L. *How to Raise an Emotionally Healthy Teenager: The Essential Guide to the New Adolescence.* New York: Dutton, 1997.

Silverstein, O., and B. Rashbaum. *The Courage to Raise Good Men.* New York: Viking, 1994.

Smith, A., J. Cooper, and M. Leverte. *Giving Kids a Piece of the Action.* TACT, 1983.

Smith, N. D. "Girls and Boys Making Connections through the Gender Relations Project." *MemberLink: A Newsletter for the Members of the Wellesley Center for Women,* Spring/Summer 1998.

Smith, R. "Schooling and the Formation of Students' Gender Identities." Paper presented at the annual conference of the American Educational Research Association, *ERIC Document 382496,* 1994.

Sokolove, M. "What Men Are Made of: Helping Boys Find New Paths to Manhood." *The Philadelphia Inquirer,* June 8, 1997 <www.phillynews.com/inquirer>.

Stone, S., and M. Roderick. "Peering into the Black of Tracking: Opportunities to Learn, Contexts, and Mathematics Achievement." Paper presented at the annual meeting of the American Educational Research Association, San Francisco, CA, April 18-22, 1995.

Tatum, B. *Why Are All the Black Kids Sitting Together in the Cafeteria?* New York: Basic Books, 1997.

The College Board. *Reaching the Top: A Report of the National Task Force on Minority High Achievement.* Princeton, NJ: The College Board, 1999.

The Commonwealth Fund. "The Health of Boys." *Education Week,* July 8, 1998:4.

The Mid-Atlantic Equity Center. *Positive Parenting: The Law of Return.* Chevy Chase, MD: MAEC, 1998.

The National Coalition of Educational Equity Advocates. *Educate America: A Call for Equity in School Reform.* Chevy Chase, MD: The Mid-Atlantic Equity Consortium, 1994.

Tukufu, D. *A Guide Toward The Successful Development of African- American Males.* Richmond Heights, OH: Tukufu Group, 1997.

Thompson, C. "Education and Masculinity." A. Carelli, Ed. *Sex Equity in Education: Readings and Strategies.* (47-54). Springfield, IL: Charles C. Thomas Publisher, 1988.

Thompson, M. "Boys to Men: Questions of Violence." *Harvard Education Letter Research Online* (Forum Feature July/August 1999), August 10, 1999 <www.edletter.org/forum>.

U.S. Census Bureau. "Children with Single Parents: How They Fare." November 1, 1999 <www.census.gov/prod/www/titles.html>.

————. Unpublished Tables. "Marital Status and Living Arrangements: March 1998." November 1, 1999. <www.census.gov/prod/99pubs/p20-514u.pdf>.

U.S. Department of Education. *Digest of Education Statistics.* Washington, DC: USDOE, 1997a.

————. *Dropout Rates in the United States.* Washington, DC: USDOE, 1996a.

————. *National Assessment of Educational Progress, The 1994 High School Transcript Study Tabulations.* Washington, DC: USDOE, 1996b.

————. Office for Civil Rights, *National Summaries from the Elementary and Secondary School Civil Rights Survey.* Washington, DC: USDOE, 1994.

————. *Students' Peer Groups in High School: The Pattern of Relationship to Educational Outcomes.* Washington, DC: USDOE, 1997b.

U.S. Department of Health and Human Services, Centers for Disease Control and Prevention, National Center for Chronic Disease, Prevention and Health Promotion, Division of Adolescent and School Health, *The Youth Risk Behavior Surveillance System.* Washington, DC: U.S. Government Printing Office, 1995.

U.S. Department of Justice, Office of Justice Programs. *Juvenile Delinquents in the Federal Criminal Justice System.* Washington, DC: U.S. Department of Justice, 1997.

————. *Juvenile Felony Defendants in Criminal Courts.* Washington, DC: U.S. Department of Justice, 1998.

————. "Young Black Male Victims." *National Crime Victimization Survey.* Washington, DC: U.S. Department of Justice, 1994.

Walker-Moffat, W. *The Other Side of the Asian American Success Story.* San Francisco: Jossey-Bass, 1995.

Walters, M. Interview with L. Gordon, November 9, 1998.

Walters, M., et. al. *The Invisible Web: Gender Patterns in Family Relationships.* New York: Guilford Press, 1992.

Bibliography

Biology

Begley, S. "Your Child's Brain." *Newsweek,* February 19, 1996.

Fausto-Sterling, A. *Myths of Gender: Biological Theories about Women and Men.* New York: Basic Books, 1985.

Goleman, D. *Emotional Intelligence.* New York: Bantam Books, 1995.

Gorman, C. "How Gender May Bend Your Thinking." *Time,* July 17, 1995:44.

Moir, A., and D. Jessel. Brain Sex: *The Real Difference Between Men and Women.* New York: Carol Publishing, 1991.

Ornish, D. *Love and Survival.* New York: Harper-Collins, 1997.

Gender Studies

Abbott, F., Ed. *Boyhood: Growing Up Male, A Multicultural Anthology.* Freedom, CA: Crossing Press, 1993.

Bell, D. *Being a Man: The Paradox of Masculinity.* Vermont: The Lewis Publishing Company, 1982.

Betcher, W. *A Time of Fallen Heroes: The Re-Creation of Masculinity.* New York:Guilford Press, 1995.

Biddulph, S. *Raising Boys.* Berkeley, CA: Ten Speed Press, 1998.

Bly, R. Iron John: *A Book About Men.* Reading: Addison-Wesley, 1990.

Bushweller, K. "Turning Our Backs on Boys." *The American School Board Journal,* May 1994:20-25.

Capital Area School Development Association, School of Education. *Men Helping Boys with Difficult Choices.* Albany: State University of New York Press, 1996.

Connell, R. *Teaching the Boys: New Research on Masculinity and Gender Strategies for Schools.* Sydney: Teachers College Record, 1996.

Costello, C., S. Miles, and A. Stone, Eds. *The American Woman 1999-2000: A Century of Change — What's Next?* New York: W.W. Norton and Company, 1998.

Enger, J. "Internal/External Locus of Control and Parental Verbal Interaction of At-Risk Adolescent Black Males." Paper presented at the annual meeting of the American Educational Research Association, *ERIC Document 360453,* 1993.

Fivush, R. "Exploring Sex Differences in the Emotional Content of Mother-Child Conversation About the Past." *Sex Role,* 20(11/12):675-691, 1989.

Garbarino, J. *Lost Boys: Why Our Sons Turn Violent and How We Can Save Them.* New York: The Free Press, 1999.

Gerzon, M. *A Choice of Heroes: The Changing Faces of American Manhood.* Boston: Houghton Mifflin, 1992.

Gilligan, C., N. Lyons, and T. Hanmer. *Making Connections: The Relational Worlds of Adolescent Girls at Emma Willard School.* Boston: Harvard University Press, 1990.

Gilligan, J. Violence: *Reflections on a National Epidemic.* New York: Vintage Books, 1997.

Gurian, M. *The Wonder of Boys.* New York: Tarcher/Putnam, 1996.

———. *A Fine Young Man.* New York: Putnam, 1998.

Henderson, N. "What Makes School Good for Boys?" *The Washington Post,* January 8, 1999:6-8.

Herzog, J., and E. Herzog. "Gender." *Sesame Street Parents,* December 1994: 47-52.

Hornblower, M. "Beyond the Gender Myths." *Time,* October 19, 1998:90-1.

Jones, R. "I Don't Feel Safe Here Anymore: Your Legal Duty to Protect Gay Kids from Harassment." *The American School Board Journal,* November 1999: 26-31.

Jordan, E. "Fighting Boys and Fantasy Play: The Construction of Masculinity in the Early Years of School." *Gender and Education,* 7(1):69-86, 1995.

Kenworthy, T. "'Help Us Heal,' Clinton Urges Columbine." *The Washington Post,* May 21, 1999:A15.

Kimmel, M. *Manhood in America.* New York: S&S Trade, 1997.

Kimmel, M., and M. Messner, Eds. *Men's Lives.* New York: MacMillan, 1992.

Kindlon, D., and M. Thompson. *Raising Cain: Protecting the Emotional Life of Boys.* New York: Ballantine, 1999.

Kivel, P. *Boys Will Be Men: Raising Our Sons for Courage, Caring, and Community.* Gabriola Island, BC, Canada: New Society Publishers, 1999.

Lewin, T. "How Boys Lost Out to Girl Power." *The New York Times,* December 13, 1998:3.

Levant, R.F. *Masculinity Reconstructed: Changing the Rules of Manhood - At Work, In Relationships, and in Family Life.* New York: Dutton, 1995.

Mead, M. *Male and Female: The Classic Study of the Sexes.* New York: Quill, 1996.

Messner, M. "Boyhood, Organized Sports, and the Construction of Masculinities." *Journal of Contemporary Ethnography,* 18(4):416-444, 1990.

————. *Politics of Masculinities: Men In Movements.* Thousand Oaks, CA: Sage Publications, 1997.

Messner, M., and D. Sabo. *Sex, Violence and Power in Sports: Rethinking Masculinity.* Freedom, CA: The Crossing Press, 1994.

Norman, M. "From Carol Gilligan's Chair." *The New York Times Magazine,* November 9, 1997:50.

Parker, A. "The Construction of Masculinity within Boys' Physical Education." *Gender and Education,* 8(2):141-57, 1996.

Phillips, A. *The Trouble With Boys.* New York: Harper Collins, 1993.

Phillips, L. *The Girls Report: What We Know and Need to Know About Growing Up Female.* New York: The National Council for Research on Women, 1998.

Rosenfeld, M. "Little Boys Blue: Reexamining the Plight of Young Males." *The Washington Post,* March 26, 1998:A1.

Sadker, M., and D. Sadker. Failing at Fairness: *How America's Schools Cheat Girls.* New York: Scribners, 1994.

Salisbury, J., and D. Jackson. *Challenging Macho Values: Practical Ways of Working With Adolescent Boys.* London: Falmer Press, 1995.

Segal, L. *Slow Motion: Changing Masculinities, Changing Men.* New Jersey: Rutgers University Press, 1990.

Shaffer, S., and L. Shevitz. "She Bakes and He Builds: Gender Bias in the Curriculum." *Double Jeopardy: Addressing Gender Bias in Special Education Services.* Albany, NY: State University of New York Press, 1999.

Skelton, C. "Learning to be 'Tough': The Fostering of Maleness in One Primary School." *Gender and Education,* 8(2):185-97, 1996.

Smith, N. "Girls and Boys Making Connections Through the Gender Relations Project." *MemberLink: A Newsletter for the Members of the Wellsley Center for Women,* Spring/Summer 1998.

Smith, R. "Schooling and the Formation of Students' Gender Identities." Paper presented at the annual conference of the American Educational Research Association, *ERIC Document 382496,* 1994.

The Commonwealth Fund. "The Health of Boys." *Education Week.* July 8, 1998:4.

Thibert, G., and T. Karsenti. "Motivation Profile of Adolescent Boys and Girls: Differences Throughout Schooling." Paper presented at the annual conference of the American Educational Research Association, *ERIC Document 395248,* 1996.

Thompson, C. "Education and Masculinity." A. Carelli, Ed. *Sex Equity in Education: Readings and Strategies* (47-54). Springfield, IL: Charles C. Thomas Publisher, 1988.

Thorne, B. *Gender Play: Girls and Boys in School.* New Jersey: Rutgers University Press,1993.

Warren-Sams, B. "More Than a Few Good Men" *NCSEE News,* Fall 1998:2.

Weis, L. "Identity Formation and the Processes of 'Othering': Unraveling Sexual Threads" *Educational Foundations,* 9(1):17- 33, 1995.

———. "White Male Working-Class Youth: An Exploration of Relative Privilege and Loss." L. Weis and M. Fine, Eds. *Beyond Silenced Voices: Class, Race, and Gender in United States Schools.* Albany, NY: State University of New York Press, 1993.

Psychology

Albom, M. *Tuesdays With Morrie.* New York: Doubleday, 1997.

Benjamin, J. *The Bonds Of Love.* Toronto: Pantheon, 1988.

Blos, P. *On Adolescence: A Psychoanalytic Interpretation.* London: Collier-Macmillan Limited, 1962.

————. "The Second Individuation Process of Adolescence." *The Psychoanalytic Study of the Child, Vol. 22.* New York: International University Press, 1996.

Bowlby, B. *Attachment and Loss.* New York: Basic Books, 1980.

Brazelton, B., and B. Cramer. *The Earliest Relationship: Parents, Infants and the Drama of Early Attachment.* New York: Addison- Wesley, 1989.

Clines, F. "The Therapy Question." *The New York Times,* September 17, 1998 <www.nytimes.com>.

DeBaryshe, B., G. Patterson, and D. Capaldi. "A Performance Model for Academic Achievement in Early Adolescent Boys." *Developmental Psychology,* 29(5):795-804, 1993.

Erickson E. *Identity, Youth and Crisis.* New York: W.W. Norton, 1996.

————. *Childhood and Society.* New York: W.W. Norton, 1963.

Freud, A. "Psychoanalytic Study of the Child." *Journal of Adolescence,* 1958:250-278.

Gaylin, W. *The Male Ego.* New York: Viking, 1992.

Golden, Marita. *Saving Our Sons: Raising Black Children in a Turbulent World.* New York: Doubleday, 1996.

Gurian, M. *Mothers, Sons and Lovers: How a Man's Relationship with his Mother Affects the Rest of His Life.* Boston: Shambhala Publications, 1994.

Harris, J. *The Nurture Assumption.* New York: The Free Press, 1998.

Hendrix, H. *Keeping The Love You Find.* New York: Simon and Schuster, 1992.

Kantrowitz, B., and C. Kalb. "Boys Will Be Boys." *Newsweek,* May 11, 1998:54-60.

Levy,S. "Loitering on the Dark Side." *Newsweek,* May 3,1999:39.

Lichtenberg, G. *Playing Catch With My Mother: Coming to Manhood When All The Rules Have Changed.* New York: Bantam, 1999.

Meltz, B. "Boys Need Moms Too." *Boston Globe,* November 7, 1998 <www.boston.com/dailyglobe>.

Miller, J., and I. Stiver. Healing Connection: How Women Form Relationships in Therapy and in Life. Boston: Beacon Press, 1997.

Norman, M. "From Carol Gilligan's Chair." *New York Times Magazine,* November 9, 1997:50.

Parke, R., and A. Brott. *Throwaway Dads.* Boston: Houghton Mifflin and Co., 1999.

Pollack, W. Real Boys: *Rescuing our Sons from the Myths of Boyhood.* New York: Random House, 1998.

Real, T. *I Don't Want to Talk about It: Overcoming the Secret Legacy of Male Depression.* New York: Simon and Schuster, 1997.

———. Keynote Presentation at The Family Network Conference, Washington, DC: March 1998.

Shem, S., and J. Surrey. *We Have to Talk: Healing Dialogues Between Women and Men.* New York: Basic Books, 1998.

Siegler, A. "How to Raise an Emotionally Healthy Teenager." *The Essential Guide to the New Adolescence.* New York: Dutton, 1997.

Silverstein, O., and B. Rashbaum. *The Courage to Raise Good Men.* New York: Viking, 1994.

Stoltenberg, J. *The End of Manhood: A Book for Men of Conscience.* New York: Dutton, 1993.

Taffel, R. *Why Parents Disagree: How Women and Men Parent Differently and How We Can Work Together.* New York: William Morrow and Company, 1994.

Walters, M. *The Invisible Web: Gender Patterns in Family Relationships.* New York: Guilford Press, 1992.

Wolin, S., and S. Wolin. *The Resilient Self.* New York: Villard Books, 1993.

Race/Ethnic Studies

Abbott, F., Ed. *Boyhood: Growing Up Male, A Multicultural Anthology.* Freedom, CA: Crossing Press, 1993.

Brettel, C., and C. Sargent, Eds. *Gender in Cross-Cultural Perspective.* New Jersey: Prentice-Hall, Inc., 1993.

Bush V, L. *Can Black Mothers Raise Our Sons?* Chicago: African American Images, 1999.

Comer, J., and A. Poussaint. *Raising Black Children: Two Leading Psychiatrists Confront The Educational, Social, and Emotional Problems Facing Black Children.* New York: Plume, 1992.

Connell, R. "Disruptions: Improper Masculinities and Schooling." L. Weis and M. Fine, Eds. *Beyond Silenced Voices: Class, Race, and Gender in United States Schools* (191-385). Albany: State University of New York Press, 1993.

Hendrie, C. "Failing But Feeling Fine: Black Male Teenagers' Esteem is not Linked to Academic Achievement." *Teacher Magazine,* 1998:24.

Hill, P. "Coming of Age: African American Male Rites of Passage." *ERIC Document 356284,* 1992.

King, A. "Turning Boys to Men: Community-Based Programs for At-Risk Young Black Males are Highlighted at a Joint Center Conference." *Focus,* August 1994:3-4.

Lee, E. *Ten Principles on Raising Chinese American Teens.* San Mateo, CA: AACP Inc., 1987.

Marchetti, G. Romance and the *"Yellow Peril:" Race, Sex, and Discursive Strategies in Hollywood Fiction.* San Mateo, CA: AACP Inc., 1994.

Mincy, R., Ed. *Young Black Males: Challenges to Agencies, Programs, and Social Policy.* Washington, DC: The Urban Institute Press, 1994.

Osborne, J. "Race and Academic Disidentification." *Journal of Educational Psychology,* 89(4):728-35, December 1997.

Polite, V., and J. Davis, Eds. *African American Males in School and Society: Practices and Policies for Effective Education.* New York: Teachers College Press, 1999.

Perez, S. *Moving From the Margins: Puerto Rican Young Men and Family Poverty.* Washington, DC: National Council of La Raza, 1993.

Stecopoulos, H., and M. Uebel, Eds. *Race and the Subject of Masculinities.* Raleigh-Durham: Duke University Press, 1997.

Turner, T., and K. McFate. "Programs That Serve Young Black Males: A Statistical Study Conducted by the Joint Center Shows That Programs Serving Young Black Males Are Generally Underfunded." *Focus,* August 1994:5-7.

Yun, G., Ed. *A Look Beyond the Model Minority Image: Critical Issues in Asian America.* San Mateo, CA: AACP, Inc., 1989.

Sociology

Adams, B. "Change and Continuity in the U.S. Family Today." *Bangladesh Journal of Sociology,* 1998.

Barnard, L. "For Crying Out Loud." *The Toronto Sun,* February 23, 1998 <www.thepaperboy.com>.

Begley, S. "It's Time to Rethink Nature Versus Nurture." *Newsweek,* March 27, 1995:48-54.

Britt, D. "Tough Lessons Behind the Wheel." *The Washington Post,* July 17, 1998:C1.

Children Now. "Boys to Men: Entertainment Media - Messages About Masculinity." November 10, 1999 <www.childrennow.org>.

———. "Boys to Men: Sports Media - Messages About Masculinity." November 10, 1999 <www.childrennow.org>.

Cohen, S. "The Drinking Age." *The Washington Post Magazine,* June 7, 1998:10.

Cohn, D. "Single Father Households on the Rise." *The Washington Post,* December 11, 1998:A-1,6-7.

Coontz, S. *The Way We Really Are: Coming to Terms With America's Changing Families.* New York: Harper Collins, 1997.

Engber, A., and L. Klungness. *The Complete Single Mother.* Holbrook, MA: Adams Media Corporation, 1995.

Griswold, R. *Fatherhood in America: a History.* New York: Basic Books, 1993.

Gutkind, L. *Stuck in Time.* New York: Henry Holt and Company, 1993.

Hart, D. "What About Our Boys?" *Maryland Statewide Equity News and Voices,* Spring 1998:1,3.

Levine, J., and T. Pittinsky. *Working Fathers: New Strategies for Balancing Work and Family.* New York: Addison-Wesley Publishing Co., 1997.

Messner, M., and D. Sabo. *Sex, Violence and Power in Sports: Rethinking Masculinity.* Freedom, California: The Crossing Press, 1994.

Messner, M. "Boyhood, Organized Sports, and the Construction of Masculinities." *Journal of Contemporary Ethnography,* 18(4):416-444, 1990.

Miedzian, M. *Boys Will Be Boys: Breaking the Link Between Masculinity and Violence.* New York: Doubleday, 1991.

Niehoff, D. *The Biology of Violence.* New York: The Free Press, 1999.

Nerburn, K. *Letters To My Son: A Father's Wisdom on Manhood, Women, Life and Love.* San Rafael, CA: New World Library, 1994.

Osherson, S. *The Passions of Fatherhood.* New York: Ballantine Books, 1995.

Palladino, G. *Teenagers: An American History.* New York: Harper Collins, 1996.

Perlstein, L. "Tough Subject: Lowering Latino Dropout Rate." *The Washington Post,* December 1, 1998:A3.

Parrow, A. "Race, Father Absence and the Educational Ambition of Adolescent Males." *ERIC Document 148984,* 1977.

Pittman, F. *Man Enough: Fathers, Sons and the Search for Masculinity.* New York: G.P. Putnam and Sons, 1993.

————. "The Masculine Mystique." *Networker,* 14(3):40-45, May/June 1990.

Prothrow-Stith, D., and M. Weissmann. *Deadly Consequences: How Violence is Destroying Our Teenage Population and a Plan to Begin Solving The Problem.* New York: Harper Collins, 1991.

Reilly, R. "The Good Father" *Sports Illustrated,* September 7, 1998:32-45.

Rofes, E. "Making Schools Safe for Sissies." *Rethinking Schools,* 9(3):8-9, 1995.

Shapiro, L. "Guns and Dolls." *Newsweek,* May 28, 1998:56-65.

Viadero, D. "Carol Gilligan: On Assignment." *Education Week,* May 13, 1998: 35-38.

Statistics

American Association of University Women. *Hostile Hallways: The AAUW Survey on Sexual Harassment in America's Schools.* Washington, DC: AAUW, 1993.

————. *Separated By Sex: A Critical Look at Single-Sex Education for Girls.* Washington, DC: AAUW, 1998.

American Youth Policy Forum. *The Forgotten Half Revisited.* Washington, DC: AYPF, 1998.

Anderson, R., K. Kochanek, and S. Murphy. *Report of Final Mortality Statistics.* Washington, DC: Centers for Disease Control and Prevention, 1995.

Centers for Disease Control and Prevention. *Monthly Vital Statistics Report,* 45(11)S2:57, 1997.

Moore, J. "Going Down to the Barrio: Homeboys and Homegirls in Change." *ERIC Document 393622,* 1991.

National Institute on Drug Abuse. "High School and Youth Trends." *Monitoring the Future Study,* 1996.

National Institute of Mental Health. "Suicide Facts, 1996." December 12, 1999. <www.nimh.gov/research/suifact.htm>.

SRI. *National Longitudinal Transition Study of Special Education Students.* Menlo Park, CA: SRI International, 1993.

U.S. Department of Education. *Annual Report on School Safety.* Washington, DC: USDOE, 1998.

————. *Digest of Education Statistics.* Washington, DC: USDOE, 1997.

————. *Dropout Rates in the United States.* Washington, DC: USDOE, 1996.

————. *National Assessment of Educational Progress, the 1994 High School Transcript Study Tabulations.* Washington, DC: USDOE, 1996.

————. Office for Civil Rights, *National Summaries from the Elementary and Secondary School Civil Rights Survey.* Washington, DC: USDOE, 1994.

————. *Students' Peer Groups in High School: The Pattern of Relationship to Educational Outcomes.* Washington, DC: USDOE, 1997.

U.S. Department of Health and Human Services, Centers for Disease Control and Prevention, National Center for Chronic Disease, Prevention and Health Promotion, Division of Adolescent and School Health. *The Youth Risk Behavior Surveillance System.* Washington, DC: U.S. Government Printing Office, 1995.

U.S. Department of Justice, Office of Justice Programs. *Juvenile Delinquents in the Federal Criminal Justice System.* Washington, DC: U.S. Department of Justice, 1997.

————. *Juvenile Felony Defendants in Criminal Courts.* Washington, DC: U.S. Department of Justice, 1998.

————. "Young Black Male Victims." *National Crime Victimization Survey.* Washington, DC: U.S. Department of Justice, 1994.

About the Authors

Susan Morris Shaffer is currently the Deputy Director of The Mid-Atlantic Equity Center. Ms. Shaffer is nationally recognized for her work in the development of comprehensive technical assistance and training programs on educational equity and gender-related issues. She has authored or co-authored several publications related to gender equity, mathematics and science education, women's history, multicultural education, and disability. She has managed a number of grants from the U.S. Department of Education's Women's Educational Equity Act Program and has spent 30 years both teaching and working in public schools. Ms. Shaffer holds an undergraduate degree in history and a graduate degree in education from the University of California, Berkeley.

Linda Perlman Gordon, LCSW-C, M.Ed., is a clinical social worker and a trained mediator. She has directed a court-mandated parenting seminar for divorcing parents, and as a member of the Montgomery County Divorce Roundtable, developed the Supervised Visitation Program for Montgomery County, MD. She is a graduate of The Family Therapy Practice Center, has advanced degrees in Social Work and Education, and is a member of the Board of Trustees of the Clinical Social Work Institute. Ms. Gordon has taught seminars on the subjects of divorce and blended families, trained seminar leaders, and developed programs concerning mental health issues for children. She has a private psychotherapy practice in Washington, DC treating individuals, couples, and families.